FIND FULFILLMENT
THROUGH PROSPERITY
FROM JAPAN'S
FATHER OF MANAGEMENT

THE
PATH

KONOSUKE MATSUSHITA

New York Chicago San Francisco Lisbon London Madrid Mexico City
Milan New Delhi San Juan Seoul Singapore Sydney Toronto

The **McGraw·Hill** Companies

1 2 3 4 5 6 7 8 9 10 11   WFR/WFR   1 9 8 7 6 5 4 3 2 1 0

ISBN   978-0-07-173957-3
MHID   0-07-173957-2

Library of Congress Cataloging-in-Publication Data

Matsushita, Konosuke, 1894–1989.
    [Michi o hiraku. English]
        The path / by Konosuke Matsushita.
            p.   cm.
        ISBN-13: 978-0-07-173957-3 (alk. paper)
        ISBN-10: 0-07-173957-2 (alk. paper)
        1. Conduct of life.   2. Businesspeople—Conduct of
life.   3. Matsushita, Konosuke, 1894–1989.   I. Title.

BJ1595.M313   2010
650.1—dc22   2010018934

CONTENTS

I

The Path

■ □ ■

*When it rains, we casually put up an
    umbrella.*
*We rarely stop to think about such an
    instinctive response.*
It comes naturally.
In our simplest, most unconscious responses,
We can observe fundamental principles
About the ways the world works best.
We can grasp basic truths,
And we can gain tremendous strength.
Stopping to think with a free and open mind
*About the state of our world and about our
    work,*
We can find in these simple, natural responses
The path we should take as human beings
And the path our country should follow.

■ □ ■

OUR PATH

Each of us has a path that is ours and ours alone to follow. That path is our own life, precious and heaven-sent. We don't really know where this path will take us, but we know no one else will ever have one exactly like it. For each of us, it is our own personal path, and it is one we will never travel down a second time. Our way takes us through wide, open spaces but also into narrow, tight spots. The path ascends, carrying us high at one time, but at other times, it descends, bringing us down. The way is sometimes smooth, and we stride forth unencumbered, but at others we must clear obstacles from our way, struggling with each step.

There are times when we are at our wit's end, unsure as to whether the path is a good one or bad. There are times when we want to take a detour. But ultimately, there is no other way for us than the path that we are on.

It is not a matter of just meekly resigning ourselves, but the important thing is we must keep going along the path we are on. Isn't it the path that we and only we can travel, the life that is uniquely and irreplaceably ours?

We may gaze in envy at the lives of others, and we may be stymied, but we cannot see which way to go. For our way to open up, what we have to do is to keep going, to keep moving along. We have to make up our minds and be resolute, to the best of our ability. The journey may seem long, but when we stride forth, without pause, our path will open up and will lead to happiness.

ACCEPT WHAT COMES

Adversity is the invaluable experience that tests the individual. People who have stood up to the trials of life are tough indeed. The great figures of history are those who have been buffeted by adversity and whose dauntless spirit has helped them overcome countless difficulties. Hardship is indeed precious, but to think so highly of the value of adversity that one cannot imagine human beings perfecting themselves without it is off the mark as well—a distortion. Yes, adversity is valuable, but so is smooth sailing. What matters most is whether—either in hardship or in comfort—one accepts one's circumstances for what they are. We must never forget to be humble.

When we lose our capacity for acceptance, adversity will make us mean-spirited, and comfort will render us conceited. It matters little whether those circumstances are good or bad; they are in a way the destiny given in our life. We should simply do our best to cope with the way conditions are.

Such acceptance gives human beings strength; it makes us good and wise. People who have accepted and endured their hardships and people who have continued to grow in a favorable environment have taken very different paths, but they possess a similar strength, rectitude, and wisdom.

We should all try first to accept the circumstances in which we find ourselves, without being confined by them and without indulging in either self-pity or complacence, and then do our best within those circumstances.

An Aspiration That Inspires

We should all have a dream—a goal to aspire to. And we should fervently seek to attain it. We should make it a compelling goal, one that is as important as life itself. Once you have given shape to your aspirations, you are already halfway to achieving them.

Anyone can have a dream, no matter what the person's age, and the path will open up to anyone, young or old, who is pursuing a dream. Perhaps, over the course of your life so far, you have had a goal you were seeking, but each time you sought it, you lost your path and finally had to abandon it. The fact that you could not find the path and that it did not open for you may mean that the spirit of your quest was weak. In other words, your efforts toward the goal you wanted to achieve were somehow lacking in intensity and commitment.

Do not think regretfully about the past. Make no complaint about the irretrievable months and days you have invested. And if until now you have relied on others or expected them to get you out of trouble when life got tough, you should bravely sweep the slate clean. What is important is that you seek your goal on your own. What matters is your own attitude. No matter what others may say, you must carry on, passionately, toward your goal. You must yourself show what you can do.

We should all have a dream—for ourselves, for those around us, for our countries, and for the world.

FEELING OUR WAY

There is much we can learn from those whose vision is impaired. Although they cannot see the world clearly, they rarely get hurt. Meanwhile, those with ordinary vision often trip, bump into doorjambs, and stumble or hit themselves. They tend to take their sight for granted, forgetting to be careful, and it leaves them open to injury.

The sight-impaired, however, grope their way. They take every step with care. They are humble and cautious. And all their senses are focused with every step they take. No sighted person ever proceeds as carefully and consciously.

If you want to avoid getting hurt in life, if you want to avoid social stumbles and falls, you should take a hint from the sight-impaired. Even knowing full well that calamity can be only a step away, the way we conduct ourselves is often rash and ill-considered.

No matter how old we are, there are aspects of life we will not understand. That is the way of the world. That being so, there is no other way but to proceed with care. Nothing is more dangerous than to go through life assuming that you understand everything. Rather, we should think we do not understand at all and let others teach us and lead us by the hand, moving forward step-by-step with humility and commitment. Together we should feel our way carefully through life.

FOLLOW NATURE

There is a natural time and season for everything in nature. Flowers blossom in spring; leaves wither and fall in winter. Flowers and grasses, trees, vegetables, and fruit grow anew during the growing season and bear fruit or seeds, each in its own season. When that season is over, they wither and die. In the course of their existence, there is no self-interest, no ambition; they are selfless and open. So nature is beautiful and order prevails.

With human beings, however, life does not go so smoothly. Humans do not meekly submit to nature and tend always to cling to something or some idea. They tend to develop ambitions and react on random and personal impulses. So they quickly develop discontents and lose sight of nature's laws. They initiate action at the wrong time and err in their direction. And peace and order is disturbed.

When flowers bloom at odd seasons, they are considered oddities. They have appeared at the wrong time. In a flower, such anomalies have the attraction of being rare, but this may not apply to human beings. A human being who has taken a wrong course cannot be taken lightly. Such a person can be hurt and can cause trouble for others.

Nothing is as difficult as assuring that one does not err in one's course of action. It is all the more valuable to take nature as one's teacher, pausing from time to time to examine a blossom and to hold a flower of the field in one's hand, contemplating the laws of nature and the management of one's self.

DIFFERENCES ARE GOOD

In early spring the flowers bloom, and by early summer the trees are bright with fresh foliage; the landscape of hills and fields comes to its full splendor. The greater the varieties of flowers, the more diverse the trees and shrubs in bud, the more numerous the species of birds in skies, the more stunning the scene. This is the panoply of nature.

If there were nothing but cherry blossoms as far as the eye could see, or vast expanses of nothing but cedar trees, or if there were nothing but warblers everywhere—though these creatures do have their special charms—we probably would not think of the landscape as especially beautiful or abundant.

Fortunately, there are all manner of flowers, and the forests are mixed and diverse all over the archipelago, and there are countless species of birds, all thanks to the laws of nature. Human beings, too, are diverse. Precisely because there are so many different kinds of people, they can do multifarious varieties of work. You are different not only in looks but in temperament from other people. Your likes and dislikes are different. All that is good. Differences are not to be lamented. Rather, we should see in them infinite attraction and potential; we should find in them infinite bounty. Each and every person should be able to work to his or her potential, and all people should help each other.

Thank goodness for human diversity. Thank goodness each and every person is so different.

ONE MOUNTAIN AFTER ANOTHER

"My journey's path, one mountain after another . . ."

I've long forgotten where I heard this verse or where I read it, but this one line alone has remained with me, floating back into my mind now and then.

Just as you have reached the summit of one mountain in your journey and caught your breath, there lies before you another mountain. You trudge upward, gaining the next peak, and there lies yet another ridge, endlessly, endlessly along the path.

This is one of the truths of our lives as well. And truth as it is, none of us can avoid the endless succession of challenges that lie before us. Inasmuch as we cannot avoid them, we should negotiate each mountain as best we can.

High peaks; low ridges; barren, stormy crags; gentle, rounded hillocks—people's varied lives form a rich fabric woven over diverse terrain, and the traces of our paths leave the imprints of where we have traveled. Sometimes the rain must fall and storms must rage, and we drag ourselves with heavy steps along our way. But then we may be blessed with warmth and sunshine, and the chirping of birds will cheer us.

We must persevere with energy and spirit along the way, gaining each peak that rises before us and traveling as far as we can go. Each mountain, successfully climbed, whets our ambition to challenge another.

FIGHTING WITH REAL SWORDS

In fencing, we protect ourselves with a head protector, gloves, and a breastplate, and we fight with bamboo swords. We may enter into the fray as if fighting for real, but inevitably, we are not completely on our guard. We know we won't die if we are struck, that we won't even shed blood. If we replace the bamboo practice sword with one made of hardwood as we face an opponent, the level of tension rises considerably. If the hardwood sword hits home, you could be knocked out, you could get hurt—indeed, you could be killed.

All the more, if opponents face each other with real swords, the life of one or the other could be over in an instant. There is no room for easy, winsome/lose-some notions. There are only two possible outcomes: one wins, one loses. The one who loses, dies. This is the nature of fighting with real swords.

Life itself is essentially a fight with a real sword: you take your life in your hands whatever you do. No matter how small the matter, you have to undertake it as if your life depended on it. There is no need to feel overly constrained, but you should not indulge yourself with facile win-some/lose-some rationalizations. You might comfort yourself with such words after you fail, but you cannot start out in such a careless frame of mind. The course of your life is determined each time you make a decision to "use real swords" or not.

It is your own precious life you are living—valuable beyond price. Even now, it is not too late: let us renew our resolve to live each day as if we are fighting with real swords.

WHAT COMES BEFORE GOOD AND BAD

Nature has its mountains, rivers, and seas, and all of it is governed by an unknown power. The living creatures in nature, moreover—the birds, the dogs, the human beings—are all part of what we might call destiny.

Our Earth, in union with the life that unfolds upon it, exists quite apart from whether it is good or bad, right or wrong. It is part of the way life is. Among human beings as well, when we look at each individual, we can see how we all have different traits and destinies. Some are born with beautiful voices, some with the power to calculate quickly. Some can work dexterously with their hands; others are clumsy by nature. There are the stout and strong as well as the weak and frail. One might say that of the factors in a person's life, 90 percent are already determined by powers beyond human comprehension. Only 10 percent remain over which human beings can exercise control through their intellect and talent.

If we look at life from this perspective, it can help us avoid overconfidence when circumstances go well and despair when they go badly, and to move forward calmly and steadily. It can help us open up our own path with an open and humble mind. There are many ways of thinking about life, but this is one perspective that we should keep in mind.

What Illness Teaches

Many have had the experience of getting over one illness or another and glorying briefly in good health, only to fall sick once more. We can hardly expect to get through life without encountering health problems at some point or other. While the seriousness of the ailment may vary, all of us find ourselves sick in bed a number of times in the course of our lives.

Some may know illness only about five times in their whole lives, while others encounter it frequently, one affliction after another. From the colds, fevers, and contagions of childhood on to the crippling maladies of old age, each of us must endure and overcome an ailment several times in our lives.

Death, by contrast, we meet only once, and when we think about it, as often as we get sick, only once does illness end in death. Illness, therefore, can be considered part of the tests of our lives, an experience that further improves and strengthens us.

We do not know when sickness might lead to death, but if we leave that up to fate and think of the illness we currently suffer as part of the ordinary ordeal of life, it takes on new meaning. This open-minded, positive approach, along with the effects of medical care and medicines, is sure to speed us on along the path to recovery.

We should cultivate a willingness to appreciate the experience of illness. And we should take good care of ourselves when we are ill.

LIFE AND DEATH

In a way, every day of one's life is part of one's journey toward death. Life and death are all part of nature's timeless cycle, and all living creatures travel this unalterable path through life to death.

Among living creatures, only human beings have the power to cognitively grasp this law of nature and prepare themselves for the ultimate end of the journey. While never knowing when death will come, they can come up with various ideas, plans, and dreams about what they want to do during the rest of their lives. Not only those of advanced age, but young people as well, make all sorts of plans for their future, and these are, in a way, plans for death. Life and death are inseparable, so preparations for life are preparations for death.

Human beings instinctively fear death. But what we should fear more than death itself is facing death without having prepared ourselves for it. We are always face-to-face with death—indeed, that is what makes life so precious. And precisely because of death's constant imminence, we must make the very best we can of the life that is given us. Thinking about how to make the best of life is a form of planning for death, and thereby planning of one's life.

All of us must face squarely the stern fate assigned to all living creatures and consider solemnly, as well as with anticipation, how we can make our lives meaningful and full.

2

To Greet Each Day as a New Day

■ □ ■

How can we foster youthfulness and dynamism in our country? Our region? Our community? All working people, students, executives, homemakers—everyone in every occupation—can emerge anew, shedding old skins and moving forth, out into new horizons. It is time to think seriously, with courage and commitment, about how to set ourselves upon the path to genuine peace, happiness, and prosperity.

■ □ ■

Each Day Is a New Day

When the New Year comes, we feel the sense of a fresh start, an embarking on a new endeavor, the turning over of a new leaf. Fresh starts, new ventures are what we celebrate, not only at New Year's but at any time.

Yesterday and today, the workings of nature follow constant laws. The sun that shines, the winds that blow are much the same, day to day. But when we are at the start of a new journey, everything we see and hear seems fresh and invigorating.

The year starts with New Year's Day, and each day begins when we awake. The dawn of the New Year seems in some way special, even though it is actually the same as any other day. If we could wake up with that sense of starting fresh every morning, then every day would be a kind of New Year. Greeting every day as a new start can help us think of it as fresh and special, a day to be celebrated.

Yesterday is yesterday. Today is today. There is no need to let the woes of yesterday weigh down our step today. Let bygones be bygones, and look well to every new day and the new turn of fortune that it brings. It is too much to dwell on the burdens of yesterday; better to meet each morning anew, each as a fresh departure.

Every new day greeted as a fresh start will be a good day. It is bright and invigorating for those who have a mind that is open, a heart that is humble, and a spirit alive with imagination and creativity.

OPEN YOUR MIND

The world is a big place. If you go through life with but a narrow perspective on this wide world, your options will soon be exhausted. Life is long, and to go through those long years looking at it in one confined way will exhaust your energy and resources.

Those whose perspective is limited are likely to err in judgment, taking wrong turns, making bad judgments, and inflicting harm on others. For the sake of our mutual benefit and prosperity, therefore, we should strive to actively broaden our horizons, striving constantly to widen our vision.

Even when we gain a perspective spanning a complete 180 degrees, we are still seeing only half of the world; ideally we want to extend our vision a full 360 degrees. When we gain true vision of our whole world, unconfined in any direction, then we will have achieved what might be called enlightenment.

It is not easy, however, to attain such an ideally broad perspective. Even a vision of 180 degrees must be considered exceptional, and most of us go from day to day with a breadth of vision probably somewhere in the realm of 15 to 20 degrees. This is why we burst out in anger, trigger conflict and dispute, and suffer anguish. Narrow-minded thinking undermines dynamism and prosperity.

Broaden your perspective. One's vision can never be too broad. What we can best do in pursuit of peace, prosperity, and happiness for ourselves and for others is to cultivate a broad perspective.

Mirror of the Heart

When we want to check our appearance, we look in a mirror. The mirror is honest; it shows us plainly as we really are. You might not be convinced when someone tells you your necktie is crooked, but when you look in the mirror, it becomes obvious. Looking in the mirror makes people see the errors of their ways and helps correct them.

We may be able to straighten our clothing and improve our appearance by looking in the mirror, but the wrinkles and twists that plague our hearts are not reflected there. People find it hard to recognize their own errors of thinking and behavior. Humanity may be forgiven, for, after all, there is no literal mirror that reflects the workings of the heart. However, if we but seek mirrors of the heart in that which surrounds us and have the humility to gaze into them, they can be found everywhere.

The trappings of our lives, the people in our circle, and everything around us reflect what is going on in our own hearts and minds. They are the mirrors of our hearts. Our hearts are reflected in everything and everyone around us, and all is linked to us.

The ancients taught us to remove the sources of our own blindness before pointing out the blindness in others. We should look around us carefully and turn a more attentive ear to the voices around us, for there we can see clearly reflected our thoughts and the rightness or wrongness of our actions.

THE BEST WE CAN DO

The old saying that human beings can only do their best, while the ultimate outcome is up to heaven, is certainly true and wise. One can only unselfconsciously do one's best, striving to the limit of human power, and beyond that only quietly wait and see what will happen. The result may live up to expectations, or it may fall short, but in either case, it is beyond our own limited powers. So as long as we have done the best a human being can do, we need not be distressed or dissatisfied, but only observe calmly what will unfold, trusting that the outcome will show us where the path will next lead us. If all people understood the value of this approach to life and if each person went about his or her work mindful of its wisdom, surely this world would be a quieter place.

People may think they can determine the outcome beforehand: if we do such-and-such, the results will be such-and-such. But the way of heaven is not based on such simplistic calculations. And if, in one's self-centeredness, one fails to take the many actions one ought to take, to naively expect life to go as planned is the height of ignorance of the way of heaven. We live out our days within a dizzying interplay of conflicting interests, so we should strive to take time out each day to reflect upon ourselves.

WHEN IT RAINS

When it rains, we put up an umbrella. If we don't have an umbrella, we might drape a towel or cloth over our heads. If we have neither, we will simply get wet.

Not having an umbrella when it rains means we have failed to pay attention to the elements of which we are a part and have been caught unprepared. It means we realized for the first time, only upon feeling the first drops of rain, that we might need an umbrella. We then think how we can prevent ourselves from getting wet the next time, and decide, as soon as the rain lets up, to get an umbrella. There is a lesson for life in this simple situation.

Obvious as it is, there are rainy days and clear days in our lives; there are days when all is going well and days when it goes badly. Nevertheless, when the weather is clear day after day for some time, we are inclined to forget that there may also be rainy days. Caught on a favorable trend, we end up going too far; we let down our guard. This, indeed, is the way human beings are.

The ancients admonished us always, "In times of peace, be mindful of times of turmoil." In anything we do, including our work, this is a valuable guide.

When it rains, we should put up an umbrella; when conditions are unfavorable, we should seek shelter. If we don't have an umbrella, there may be nothing we can do to keep from getting wet. But once the rain has stopped, we should resolve not to be caught out in the rain again and prepare ourselves properly. An umbrella to keep from getting wet, an umbrella to protect what we are doing in our work, an umbrella to shelter our lives—all are important.

READY TO CHANGE YOUR THINKING

All in the universe is constantly shifting and changing. Nothing that was yesterday was as it is today, as appearances change moment to moment, day after day. Every day, in other words, is new and fresh, and the daily cycle of birth and development forms the overarching fundamental principle of the universe.

Human beings, of course, are part of this fundamental principle. The way we look today is nothing like the way we looked yesterday; we change by the hour, time transfiguring us constantly as it passes. And human societies, likewise, are in the process of constant birth, rebirth, and change.

The same may be said of the way people think. The ancient saying that goes, literally, "The thinking of a wise sage turns thrice a day," is meant to say that the sage is always receptive to new ways of thinking—that is, ready to learn new lessons and see by fresh perspectives. It behooves us to avoid rigid ways of thinking.

We may be reluctant to change and find change unsettling. This may be part of our human nature, yet is it not a reflection of our clinging to a fixed idea? The capacity to shift our view once or twice a day is a sign of a progressive person, and changing three or four times a day is even better. Seeing change as part of constant development offers a positive approach to life.

Why?

Children are open and curious. When they don't understand something, they are quick to ask "Why?" and "Why?" over and over. And children throw themselves completely into their pursuit of the answers. They inquire enthusiastically. And when they get an answer, they think it over to the best of their ability. If they are not satisfied with the answer, they'll keep on asking, "Why? Why?" over and over.

Small children are not self-centered. They have few preconceptions or biases. What is good is good; what is bad is bad. So their perceptivity about the nature of life often shows surprising insight. This is how children grow: asking why, getting answers, pondering the answers with an open mind, and asking again and again, "Why?" And thus they grow up, one day at a time.

The same is true, in fact, of adults. If one meets each day as a new day, one is always asking why, always pursuing something new. And one is continually contemplating the answers and then seeking more whys. If we keep an open mind, free of self-interest, and if we can remain passionate and absorbed in our quest, we will find that there are questions everywhere to be asked. To live each day just as the day before and tomorrow just as today, clinging only to rigid formalities, our growth as human beings will stop, and so will the progress of society as a whole.

Prosperity is born out of our constant asking why.

Flowers in the Wilderness

The oasis in the desert is the delight of the traveler, a place of rest, revitalization, and encouragement for the onward journey. In the remote wilderness of mountains or plains, the sight of a single bravely blossoming flower inspires and consoles the lonely wayfarer.

The world we live in may not exactly be a desolate wasteland or an untamed wilderness, but our era is rife with complexity, risk, and unpredictability. People are constantly anxious and on edge, and the outlook can be as bleak as any desert or outback.

Our times being what they are, the very least we can do is to join together, helping and being helped, as we negotiate the hard places in our journeys. We should never allow our hearts to become dry and desolate; the least we can do is to strive to be resolute and true, as vital as the waters of the oasis, as brave as the lone flower blooming in the forest.

It may not be easy, but if we can take pride in the work we do and feel that our work is meaningful, it will naturally become clear what we should do and what path we should take.

No matter what the world brings, we should strive to serve society steadily, calmly, and methodically. Our example will give courage to others and inspire them in their endeavors as well.

Our own happiness, too, lies in striving to be as dauntless as the flower in the wilderness and as unsullied as the oasis spring in the desert.

REALIZING THE BEST IN YOURSELF

Human beings aspire to perfection and completion—and pray that they may attain such ideals.
That we end up competing with each other in this
endeavor may be inevitable, but often we find that
in our pursuit, we have unknowingly or unthink-
ingly inflicted unnecessary hardship on others or
ourselves. But indeed, is there any such thing as
perfection and completion?

The pine tree cannot be a cherry tree, and a cow
cannot be a horse. A pine is a pine; a cherry is a
cherry. The cow is a cow, and the horse is a horse. All
creatures in nature, though they may not be perfect
and complete in and of themselves, have their own
individual presence. All these creatures, by virtue of
their peculiar traits, working to their full potential,
complementing and influencing each other, together
bring about beauty and abundance in the larger
scheme of life.

The same is true of human beings. Even though
none of us is perfect in and of ourselves, by combining the qualities of each different person, if each

of us is striving to fulfill our best potential, we are capable of bringing about the happiness of ourselves and others as part of the greater harmony of nature. If we can accept this truth with an open mind, we will attain the humility, compassion, and gentleness of spirit that foster the readiness for cooperation. Men are men, women are women, cows moo, and horses neigh. The basic principle of prosperity is extremely simple.

PRACTICING INGENUITY IN LIFE

Whatever we face, we scrutinize the situation, seek creative solutions, and then do our best. If we fail, we can try again. If we do it over and still do not succeed, we can try yet another tack and start over once more.

If you try to do something exactly the same way every time, you will make no progress, no matter how many times you do it. Obediently following precedent has its merits, but it is also important to break with precedent and find a new and better way of approaching a task. If you try a new method, it often opens up a completely new path. Rather than fearing failure, we should fear a life where there is no innovation at all.

It is thanks to the innovations and inventions of our ancestors that we enjoy the fruits of modern life. Even in the smallest aspects of our daily lives, we can observe the traces of human ingenuity. The design of a teacup, the mechanism of a ballpoint pen, the shape of a safety pin—when you look closely at these items of everyday life, you cannot help admiring the ingenuity that went into their creation. Someone actually created something out of nothing.

Whatever we do, innovating to do things better should always be our goal. We should always be striving to do things better than we did them yesterday. And it goes for the smallest improvement—the slightest motion or technique. Even little innovations and subtle improvements of many people striving for something better accumulate, paving the way for the spread of prosperity.

3

Improving Our Lives Together

■ □ ■

Yesterday to today, today to tomorrow,
Each day we live is a new world.
The lively spirit in search of true freedom
Never lingers in the same routine or the same
   thoughts.
The discoveries of each moment, the steady
   growth of each day
Never fail to leave their mark.
If our spirits are like an ever-flowing river
And our strength is deep and enduring,
The shape of tomorrow's prosperity and peace
And the fulfillment of our own happiness
Will be realized of their own accord.

■ □ ■

LINKS AND CONNECTIONS

We are all born into this world through the workings
of karma, destiny, or fate, as it is variously described,
and we are linked to each other by all manner of
ties. To speak of such mystical concepts as karma
or fate may sound a bit old-fashioned, but the inter-
connectedness of all life across time cannot fail to
inspire our awe.

Some may believe that the connections between
one person and another are the result of the will
or purpose of individuals. That in turn leads us to
carelessly think we can, if we so decide, break away
from such bonds.

But in fact, we cannot break away so easily. The
bonds that bring people together are in reality
formed from the profound workings of karma—
links and connections that transcend what we think
of as human will or desire.

If these bonds between people in this world are
the workings of such transcendental forces, we
might do well to treat them with greater respect.
We ought to appreciate them more. Rather than

bewailing or bemoaning such ties, if we can humbly accept and appreciate them for what they are, that positive spirit will sustain us as we seek with sincerity and devotion to further strengthen such bonds.

That positive spirit can work wonders, even transforming darkness into light.

Exchanging Courtesies

A neighbor passes by, heading to work as you sweep the street in the bracing air of early morning. You exchange smiles and greetings: "Good morning!" "Good morning to you!"

We think little of such formalities, as with many other daily customs, but, in fact, they are worth treasuring. Even saying, "Wasn't it cold last night?" may be a formulaic expression, but it is a courteous way of establishing a connection with another person. "How have you been?" may be a formality, but it is a springboard for opening talk about more immediate matters or for beginning a job smoothly.

Who knows how these standard greetings began, but the fact that they have been passed down from our ancestors long ago is testimony to their usefulness in lubricating the events of our daily lives and making affairs work smoothly. Everyone accepts such conventions, and no one is likely, upon being greeted with "Chilly, isn't it?" to retort, "That won't make it warm," except perhaps as a joke.

There are many such expressions, and we would do well to make use of them to our advantage. Courteous and cheerful recognition of each other's presence is one way we can make our world a better place.

THE SPIRIT OF SERVICE

Give and receive, serve and be served—reciprocity is the way of the world. In other words, by giving what you have to others, you in turn receive an item or service of equivalent value from someone else. The world goes round, especially as far as human affairs are concerned, based on this principle.

The more you give, the greater will be the returns. But there are those who are presumptuous enough to think they can give little yet expect to receive a great deal. A world filled with such people would never prosper.

Giving is not just limited to physical objects; it includes services, care, love, attention. It involves sharing whatever you have in your power with others to the best of your ability. The clever can share their wits and intelligence, the strong their strength, the skillful their skills, the gentle and kind their caring, the scholarly their scholarship, the tradespeople their business, and so on.

Every person on this earth has within him or her heaven-sent qualities found in no other, if those qualities are expressed. What we must do is to put our own special gifts to the service of others. A society where the services are good is one in which each individual is generous in sharing what he or she has to share. In such a society, everyone is comfortable and happy.

STRENGTHS AND WEAKNESSES

Everything we do in this world—in our work and in our daily lives—we achieve through the give-and-take of people around us, joined together in a workplace or other community. For the life of that community to go forward, we have to keep many thoughts in mind, but one of the most important is to willingly understand and accept our mutual strengths and weaknesses. While working to realize our own and others' strengths as much as possible, we should strive to be kind and considerate, making up as best we can for our own and others' weaknesses.

We are not God, and nothing is more foolish than to expect any human being to be all-knowing and perfect. It is equally foolish to think too much of ourselves. The basic premise of work is helping others, and in turn, with the support and assistance of others, our work proceeds smoothly. Without an understanding and awareness of the give-and-take of our respective strengths and weaknesses, we would be nothing but a disorderly mob.

Strengths and weaknesses are part of our human destiny. Whether our destiny leads to prosperity or poverty can depend completely upon how considerate we are of these qualities in others.

TOLERANCE

We would be hard put to say categorically what kind of person is good and what kind of person is bad. But there are certainly people whom everyone would agree are not good, and such people are always among us in any era. A legendary sixteenth-century robber reputedly declared they were more numerous than "grains of sand on the seashore."

And that is the way it is with all of life. Human beings by nature seek the true, the good, and the beautiful, but no matter how long and hard they might search, the unbeautiful and the not-good do not disappear. Beauty and ugliness mix and mingle in every era and every place; indeed, their combination is fundamental to nature. It is really what makes the world go round.

Given the cohabitation of good and bad, therefore, it is essential for human beings to maintain a
certain level of tolerance of one another. We must
be patient with each other. There are many good
people, but those we are inclined to think are not
so good are always among us. If that is the nature
of the world, without a capacity for tolerance and
patience, we would soon be plunged into gloom
and be constantly bewailing the difficulties of this
world.

People gather together, both in their daily lives
and in order to pursue some work or occupation.
Inevitably, not everyone is virtuous and responsible. There are all kinds. This makes it all the more
necessary to nurture our capacity for patience and
tolerance.

LET EACH OTHER BE

Human life is precious, and respect is due to that
which is precious. While we may be keenly aware
of how much we treasure our own lives, there is a

tendency to forget how precious others' lives are to them. When people become self-absorbed, they put their own interests and desires before those of anyone else. Given human nature, this is inevitable, but it is no way to achieve prosperity for all, and it is no way to achieve the full potential of humanity.

There are times when one must restrain oneself and let others take the lead, withdraw and leave the initiative to someone else. We need to be ready to consider this option, because often it is the best way to achieve a dynamic prosperity in which others as well as yourself can flourish. The capacity for such restraint is what is most precious about humanity.

Put yourself aside, and give precedence to the other; by first allowing the other to flourish, you make it possible for yourself to flourish as well. This is the principle of live and let live, and its practice makes way for prosperity and for the emergence of peace and happiness.

The way to contribute to the prosperity of society as a whole comes down to finding in ourselves the humility and strength to let others be who they are.

Understanding Responsibility

When a situation happens that seems to be in no way connected to us, we may think we have no responsibility for what has happened. But when we think very carefully, how confident can we be that we indeed have absolutely no responsibility with regard to what has happened?

In our world, in which everything is infinitely and complexly interconnected, almost nothing can really be said to be totally unrelated to ourselves. The noble aspiration of Jesus Christ was to assume responsibility by giving up his physical life, not only for those of his circle but also for all others of his times and people of subsequent times. While that was the greatness of Christ and not a burden that any of us can expect of each other, we can at the very least take care not to shift onto others the burden of that for which we are responsible.

Dogs and cats will bite or claw members of their own kind they take a dislike to, without compunction. In this respect, human beings and animals are clearly set apart in nature. The best we can do is to appreciate that distinction and do our best not to belittle its value.

THE SERIOUS SCOLDING

Being criticized or reprimanded for what we do is not a pleasant experience for any of us. We might admit that we were wrong or inadequate, but we do not like being scolded for it. It is therefore perfectly natural that people would far prefer not ever to be scolded.

Even the one who delivers a scolding finds little satisfaction in it. It is not a chore that one likes to do, so it is also perfectly natural for people to prefer never to have to scold anyone.

But what would happen if, because of the combined unpleasantness of being scolded and scolding, mistakes and misjudgment were tolerated and poor performance permitted, and no one ever scolded or got scolded? Before we knew it, our perspectives and our judgment would become slack, introducing weaknesses and instability in our work.

Scolding and criticism driven by personal emotions, of course, are to be avoided; one must scold seriously, following a rational argument and giving persuasive reasons. Receiving such a serious scolding, moreover, is an experience we should learn to endure above and beyond personal emotions. The real worth of a person, in fact, comes forth in the wake of a scolding. We should all, therefore, take very seriously both scolding and being scolded.

ONLY HUMAN BEINGS

Much in this world is made possible through agreements or promises between people. From the time set for a date or meeting, to the terms of lending and borrowing money or materials, to corporate rules and national laws—all are important matters decided among people in order to assure that society and life in general works smoothly.

Such agreements flourish because of trust among people. Whether people keep their promises or agreements is a useful barometer indicating the level of their humanity. The same results also tell us much about a person's integrity and virtue.

Those who have no compunctions about breaking promises should circumstances become inconvenient for them can hardly be called civilized; they have lowered themselves to the level of beasts. Human beings alone are creatures capable of the sophisticated concept of agreement and of abiding faithfully by such promises.

When people's capacity to keep promises weakens, the influences appear in many dimensions of life in a society, emerging in negative ways on both the spiritual and the physical level. The impact is far greater, of course, than the inconvenience of time wasted in waiting for someone who is late. We must strive always to keep our promises.

THE PITFALLS OF NAÏVETÉ

Acquire endurance, perseverance, and knowledge; the orders of the principal and teachers should be obeyed without question; whenever the principal or teachers enter or leave the classroom, stand to greet them and see them off; stand up whenever answering a teacher and do not sit down until given permission by the teacher; honor the principal and teachers, bow courteously whenever you meet them on the street; honor your elders; be kind and gentle with the elderly, little children, and the weak, yield the path or your seat to them, and always offer assistance; do as your parents say, help them, and look after your younger brothers and sisters.

This is an excerpt from the "Rules for Students" that governed all primary and junior high schools in the Soviet Union. Students who broke these rules could be expelled from school. Similar rules, in fact, have been and still are in force in China and many other countries, including those in the West.

No matter how divergent the political philosophies that govern a regime, what people consider important in terms of the basics of human behavior is surprisingly common from one country to another. These basics concern matters that are important to all human beings, so they are rules found everywhere.

Lately, there has been a tendency to consider rules and morals disagreeable and unpleasant, but we should not be so naive as to think that anyone can do without them.

COMMUNICATION

As the ancients observed, life is like a rope of twisted straw. In the long course of a human being's life in this world, the good and the bad are intertwined; there is both the joyous and the sad. What seems at first so good turns out to be bad, and what was once bad turns out, in fact, to be good. Sometimes we realize only later that we anguished and hesitated unnecessarily when we should have gone ahead at the outset, keeping an open and humble mind. Often we are struck anew by the shallowness of received wisdom and how much human beings still have to learn.

There is little in this world that is thoroughly and incorrigibly bad, and there is also little that is entirely and perfectly good. Nevertheless, when we think life isn't going well, we are apt to shut our hearts to others, and when we think life is going smoothly, to become boastful, standing aloof from others.

When we shut our hearts to others or set ourselves apart from them, all communication is cut off, and we can neither cooperate with nor help each other. Our society will be full of closed-minded, isolated individuals.

In this rapidly changing world, we should strive always to communicate with each other, in good times as well as in bad, and always with an open mind and a humble heart, endeavoring to understand each other and lend each other support.

4

When You Have to Make Important Decisions

■ □ ■

Are we acting like genuinely responsible
*   adults?*
Have we overrated ourselves? Have we
*   underrated ourselves?*
Are we thinking seriously, with all our
*   resources,*
How to manage ourselves, on our own
*   strength,*
Resolved to do what has to be done, despite
*   the odds?*
Only with a profound sense of responsibility
*   and a vigorous will*
Can we build a nation that is good and
*   proud,*
A nation that does credit to its long history

> *And helps to build prosperity, peace, and*
>   *happiness*
> *For the whole world.*

■ ☐ ■

MAKING DECISIONS

To tread even the straightest of paths without wavering is by no means easy. It is all the more difficult
when the way branches east and west, or north and
south, and we must make choices, opting for one
direction or another.

No matter how we may hesitate, wondering
which way to go, considering the options, if all we
do is fret over the decisions, we will get nowhere.
If you are alone, it may be all right to linger when
you are at a loss about which way to go in the long
journey of life, but if you are at the head of a large
number of people, you cannot expect them all to
share the difficulties of deciding which way to go;
you have to decide quickly.

You can move ahead, or you can stay where you are, but most important is deciding which it will be. You yourself have to make the decision. Whether or not the path you have taken is the best may not be all that certain—after all, you are not omniscient— but prolonged indecision is not good for yourself or others; that alone is clear.

Determining our path through life, managing an enterprise, and even a responsibility as awesome as administering the affairs of a state are all priceless decision-making opportunities that we should embrace.

GIVING ORDERS

When you need to have a task completed by those under your direction, an important condition for achieving that goal is that your people be able to act on their own initiative in accordance with the orders given. But if they become overly accustomed to simply following orders and you find that nothing happens until orders are given, that is not a healthy situation. Passivity of that sort is not conducive to progress or development.

If people know by perceptiveness and good judgment what their leader expects of them, they will each be capable of proceeding at the proper time and in the proper way, even without being told. Their efforts have a flexibility and dynamism with the potential for endless growth and development.

To achieve that kind of dynamism, a leader has to have listened to what the followers have to say, even before any orders are issued. Listening and asking questions should come first. You need to know how your followers are different in their thinking from you, and you should talk with them sufficiently so that they see what you want to accomplish. Once you have won acceptance for a decision about to be made, then you should go ahead and make the decision work, one way or another. If those receiving the order are convinced that it is necessary, their understanding will be that much deeper and more flexible. If they do not understand what the order is for or why it is required, any effort they make to carry out the order will be rigid and lifeless.

Giving orders is by no means as easy as it might seem.

Steady Against the Wind

When the wind blows, the waves rise up. High waves rock the boat. A boat would rather not sway, but if the wind is strong and the waves are high, even the largest boat is bound to roll. If you attempt to vehemently fight the waves and press onward under rough conditions, it may be futile and could even result in disaster.

Another approach when the waves are high and the boat is rocked is to let your vessel rock freely, riding the waves as skillfully as you can. When you do so, it is important to stay calm, to keep your presence of mind. If you panic, you can lose your bearings, and you can sink a ship that need not be sunk. All must stand by their stations and calmly and conscientiously proceed with their work.

It is at times like this that a powerful capacity for cooperation emerges. In stormy times, nothing is more precious than cooperation. Panic can destroy such cooperation, so what we should fear more than the rocking boat is the breakdown of cooperation.

Good luck and bad luck come back-to-back in life. No one can predict when suddenly we may be buffeted by strong winds. The best you can do is to keep your eye calmly on those around you and make sure that all are alert and aware of changes in conditions.

FOLLOWING THROUGH

In whatever kind of work, decisions always come first. If the judgment that goes into the decisions is wrong, the work could all be wasted without achieving anything.

But none of us is God; we cannot see into the future, and no matter how we might scrutinize every possibility we can think of, it is virtually impossible to make a decision that is 100 percent accurate. Of course, we would prefer to be 100 percent correct, but it is too much to expect. Only God can know the outcome beforehand. We human beings can probably come roughly 60 percent close to accurately assessing a situation. If you can see clearly even 60 percent of how your decisions will turn out, your judgment can be considered quite good. How you make up for the rest depends upon your courage and resourcefulness.

No matter how good and accurate your judgment, if you do not have the courage and capacity to follow through on your decision, it means little at all. Courage and capability are what make it possible to achieve a 100 percent result even when the decision may be only 60 percent certain to have been the right one.

Even 60 percent certain is enough if we consider the situation at hand humbly and earnestly and equip ourselves with the courage and capacity to turn the outcome of our efforts into 100 percent success.

Beyond Immediate Gains

The old proverb that "One spooked horse can spook a herd of a thousand" touches on a phenomenon by no means limited to horses. Among human beings, too, just one person who picks up a misguided idea can easily lead many others down the wrong path. Particularly when the idea is in some way connected with personal interests or gain, it can throw off people's judgment, leading them to fix upon the small but immediate gains before them.

We have been admonished from time immemorial that greater wealth is to be had by farsightedness than from the profits immediately at hand, but still there are many whose enterprises fail because they have been blinded by the promise of short-term gain. Failure out of such blinkered greed would be minimal if it involved only one person, but in today's complex relationships among people and enterprises, a misperception at one enterprise can spread to all those linked to it, with devastating results.

The mistaken ideas of just a few shortsighted people can cause many problems, large and small. That we should avoid being fooled by the temptation of short-term gain is an endeavor we cannot repeat too often. In the final analysis, one can only appeal to people's conscience, so I will just keep on saying, over and over, in hopes that some will hear: resist the temptation of short-term gain.

GOOD INTENTIONS NOTWITHSTANDING

Quite often an idea we pursue, thinking it is a good one, turns out to produce the opposite result from what we anticipated. The reasons it does not pan out may vary—the idea itself was not well formed, or the project was poorly managed, or whatever— but if we examine the situation closely, we often discover the signs of overly intricate scheming.

Schemes, whether they are good ones or evil ones, are inherently contrivances to achieve some end. Evil schemes, of course, are not good, but even a scheme founded upon good intentions, if it is superficially conceived and degenerates into self- serving purposes, is no different from an evil plot and certainly no more desirable. In other words, when you want to achieve some objective, it is bet- ter not to *scheme* at all.

To talk of "planning with no scheme" is easy enough, but to avoid contrived plans, one has to grasp the true intention of the objective. A most advanced sort of enlightened thinking, mental rigor, and discipline is needed so one can behave in a natural way that transcends manipulation and merely personal hopes.

In the midst of our busy days and before we find ourselves facing unexpected worries, we should try to find time to reflect in quiet about the ways we approach life and consider how we can achieve our goals in ways that will rise above petty scheming and overly complex planning.

SEEING EFFORTS THROUGH TO THE END

Long ago, samurai had to administer a final blow to kill a wounded adversary. In Japan's martial culture, the samurai were guided by stern rules on this matter and followed established formalities. Leaving an enemy mortally wounded without finishing off the matter cleanly was considered shameful.

For the samurai of old, once a battle or engagement had ended, making certain of the outcome, sizing up the resulting situation, and tidying up

afterward were important parts of respectable conduct. Their upbringing from a young age was strict,
inculcating them through the activities of everyday
life with the requisite formalities, from table manners to the etiquette of greetings and salutations.
This training prepared them for the tough discipline
they would have to practice on the battlefield.

By comparison with such rigorous discipline, the
way we work today may often seem untidy and hap-
hazard. How often do we double-check everything
we do, see our efforts through to the end, and wrap
up loose ends carefully afterward?

Even when the results of a project are 99 percent
in, if one leaves the remaining 1 percent unfinished
and inconclusive, that which was accomplished
could be undone. It is always better to check over the
project once more, to be absolutely sure the job has
been completed to your satisfaction, than to remember with regret later something left unattended.

Just as the samurai would have been ashamed
not to observe the formalities of their profession,
we, too, should have enough pride in our work that
we would never leave it without following through
to the very end.

PUT INTUITION TO WORK

Swordsmen face off. Breaking the tension, the sharp blades clash and fly apart as the adversaries lunge and parry in movements too rapid for the eye to follow. The swordsmen's movements are not methodically thought out or logically reasoned. The combatants do not think to themselves one step at a time such thoughts as, "The opponent's sword came from the right side, so I'll parry to the right." Rather, observing the subtlest movement and sign, the swordsman's body springs into action, responding intuitively with a flash of movement that meets the attack instantaneously.

Some people may think intuition is not very scientific, and it is certainly hard to define, but intuition that grows out of rigorous and continued training can achieve results even more accurate and appropriate than what can be calculated scientifically. What human beings can achieve through training is tremendous.

Most of the scientific discoveries and breakthroughs of our world are the result of the superlative intuition of scientists based on long years of training resulting from their efforts to base their intuitive notions in scientific principles and apply them in practice. In essence, therefore, science and intuition are not mutually opposing at all.

The key is training, practice. We should strive to treasure and make better use of our intuition and to accumulate as much experience as we can.

THE WORLD'S TREASURES

His castle surrounded on all sides, the warlord Akechi Mitsuharu (1537–1582) decided that it was time for his final stand. However, according to a famous passage from the biography of Toyotomi Hideyoshi (*Taiko-ki*), before the battle destroyed his castle and everything in it, Mitsuharu is said to have sent out of the ramparts numerous valuable artworks and prized tea ceremony utensils, declaring to his foes, "I cannot bear to see these pieces reduced to ashes, so I give them into your keeping so that they will remain among the living. Please accept them."

He believed valuable goods belonged to those who possessed them as long as they were living. "They are not private possessions, but belong to society," he said. He considered them to be treasures of this world. Their time in the hands of one generation was short, and he prayed that these famed pieces and treasures would be passed down through the ages forever. If he were to allow the pieces to be lost in the flames of his defeat, said Mitsuhara, "I would be disgraced by posterity for deeds unworthy of our warrior traditions. I therefore entrust them to your care."

Mitsuhara has long been admired as a model of traditional rectitude for his capacity to avoid self-centeredness, making the correct and dispassionate decision amid the crisis he faced and handling chaotic circumstances with calm and circumspection.

The treasures of this world are certainly not limited to fine tea utensils and works of art. Even the work we do day-to-day—this, too, is part of the world's legacy. It helps to think of everything in this world as treasure and to think of our work as larger than just ourselves, taking to heart Mitsuhara's example from long ago.

Asking Yourself Is the Answer

Others are invariably the judges of what we do. Sometimes people praise us; sometimes they abuse us. We may be ignored, or we may be swept away by a wave of approving applause. There are many ways of looking at life and many ways of evaluating it.

The response of others can delight us, making our spirits soar, and it can plunge us into despair, dismayed by others' lack of understanding. That is the way of the world. Whichever way the scales may tip, however, there is always much we can learn from such judgments.

Perhaps even more important than others' evaluations, however, is what you yourself think of what you have done: Did I really do what was right? Was my idea, my behavior the most appropriate for the situation? Reflecting honestly and dispassionately within yourself may ultimately yield the most useful and reliable assessment.

Evaluating yourself is not easy. You must ask yourself and answer yourself, over and over, and be perfectly honest. It takes discipline and courage. If you can muster that courage, however, you will find that you have the real answers within you.

Try it again sometime: asking yourself and answering yourself. Sometimes asking yourself provides the answer.

PERSEVERANCE

Nothing, no matter how right or good it is, ever happens all at one stroke. Indeed, decisions that are made too swiftly almost always cause problems somewhere. The best way to accomplish a goal is always to take it one step at a time, based on careful consideration. The more valuable something is to you, the more important and right you believe it to be, the more patiently and assiduously you should consider your approach to achieving it.

The old saying goes, "Virtue is not left alone." One interpretation of this is that as long as what you are doing is good and right, it will eventually gain the understanding and support of others. Rarely, however, does such recognition come at once. It accumulates over time. So no matter how right you think you are, you should strive not to be so absorbed in what you are doing that you move too quickly, shunting aside others in your haste to achieve your goal. The better to test the validity of what you are trying to do, the more humble you should be, the more patiently you must persevere.

In the hurried pace of life today, when we must always be poised for action, the virtues of patience and steady, step-by-step exertion are often forgotten, but we should nevertheless do our best to remain humble and value the steady and assiduous.

Worrying and Wavering

We are by no means omnipotent, and life never goes completely as we plan or hope; there is always something to worry about or distress us. So we worry and wail; we vacillate and hesitate, unable to fully grasp the situation, unable to arrive at a decision. This happens all the time.

If you are playing a game like the Chinese board game Go and make a move you don't fully understand, it probably won't annoy anyone but yourself.

In our increasingly interconnected world, however, if you go ahead in your work without full understanding and assurance in what you are doing, you could cause grave trouble for others.

When you don't know what to do, ask others for advice. Break out of your shell, and humbly admit that you need help, and then listen carefully to what you are told. Whatever the advice you receive, if you sincerely seek to resolve your quandary, the answer can usually be found somewhere in what you hear.

We should all recognize that there is no shame in finding yourself stymied in the face of a decision and wavering over the options. Much more disgraceful is to withdraw within yourself and fail to seek out and benefit from the wisdom of others.

5

When You Face Adversity

■ □ ■

In the long span of life
There are moments when we are destined to
    stand,
Heart torn asunder, at difficult crossroads—
The future at stake.
In the course of its history,
There are momentous times when a country,
    too,
Must take a stand and choose
Between one path and another.
We need to nurture our ability
To consider calmly and clearly,
To cultivate the talents and traits
Fostered by tradition and history,
And treasure the earth on which we live.

■ □ ■

What Is Good About Worries

If there were nothing to worry about, nothing to distress or daunt us, the world would be a peaceful and comfortable place indeed. Reality, of course, rarely permits such bliss. There is always something to trouble us, something to cause us anguish or fill us with fear.

Depending on how you look at it, the world can seem full of pitfalls, perils, and gloom. Nevertheless, the obstacles and dangers—and the decisions we must deal with constantly as we move forward—can afford us a tremendous source of fulfillment as human beings; they are what imbue our lives with the deepest meaning. We can reap much more from these worries and woes if we look to them as a source of challenge and self-affirmation.

Fear not in the face of trouble; do not turn tail, but meet it head-on. There is a good side to worries: they can provide the chance to think anew and find a fresh approach. Being forced to reconsider and retrench, we find the courage to gather our forces, marshal our wisdom, and move forward boldly once more. A setback can turn out to be the source of a new journey; it can open up new paths. Ironic as it may seem, this mysterious way of the world is what gives life its limitless depth.

THE CAPACITY TO WAIT

There is a time for everything. Time is the invisible natural force over which human beings have no power. No matter how intensely we may wish it, spring will not come, the flowers will not bloom, until the proper time comes around. No matter how great may be our haste, all in life needs time to materialize. Once winter arrives, spring will eventually be on its way. Buds silently burgeon on the tree boughs, awaiting the lengthening of the days. Nature's abundance is all subject to the grand cycle of time.

Bad times pass, invariably yielding to good. People who achieve great feats know how to wait until the time is ripe. They wait patiently, quietly for the right time. Those who bide their time are like the buds of the trees in spring; they will know the moment to act. Waiting idly, however, is simply hoping for luck or a windfall. The trees in spring are constantly building their strength, preparing to bloom. Without that kind of stored-up strength, we cannot achieve what we plan to carry out.

Those whose time has not come must just wait. If we sincerely believe in the blessings of nature and have confidence that the time will come, we can use the time to build up our strength. And for those who have gradually accumulated strength, the time will certainly come for them to use it, for them to achieve their goal.

Told to be patient, people by nature tend to become all the more eager to move ahead. But nature is unmoved by selfish human sentiments. To human whim, nature is hard and cold; to those who wait, it endows them with warmth and light. We should cultivate the capacity for patience.

THE TENSION THAT FULFILLS

Imagine the animals in the zoo: they have no worries about food to eat or about harm from other animals. Nutritious food is laid before them as regularly as clockwork, and safely within their cages, they can snooze or yawn. It's a carefree life.

But animals in the zoo are surely not as content as they may seem. We have no way of knowing, but it may well be that they still dream of the days, the physical dangers notwithstanding, when they roamed free in the wild.

All of us dream of attaining a state where we would have no worries and no fears of danger or distress, of not having to work hard but having our needs fulfilled completely without effort. But would we ever find anything we intensely wanted to live for?

To face difficulties and adversities one after another, to grapple with uncertainty about which way to turn, to call on all our powers to meet and overcome the odds and put our lives on the line—is it not that sort of life that human beings find most fulfilling and full of life?

We should think about this when our courage is dimmed by difficulties.

UNPERTURBED BY TROUBLE

The world is wide, and life is long. In such a world and throughout our lives, trouble, difficulty, pain, and hardship are never far away, in greater or lesser degrees, for all of us. No one is exempt.

What should we do, how should we respond, in the face of trouble? A person's fortune can be decided depending on whether the difficulty is met head-on or shunned and avoided. To give way to perplexity, concluding that nothing can be done, gradually saps the spirit and drains away valuable resources of courage and drive. Even tasks one has always performed with the greatest of ease do not go forward as smoothly as they once did. Sometimes we are tempted by frustration to shift the blame and responsibilities to others and grow pessimistic with discontent, carving the hurt into our hearts by complaining.

If your resolve is firm enough, it is said, even the gods will yield the path. If you make little of difficulty but press onward, renewing your commitment to what you seek, hardship can even be a stepping-stone that carries you forward. All depends upon how you look at the situation, how strong your resolve, and how unperturbed you are by trouble.

The human spirit, like the almighty staff of the mythic Monkey King, can extend or withdraw at will. Placing our trust in such resilience, we should commit ourselves firmly to opening up our dreams, difficult as the times may be.

What Society Means to You

Society is both harsh and kind. People of old once aptly described this in now somewhat old-fashioned terms: "For every thousand who see, one thousand are blind."

There is much that society does not see and scrutinize. Poorly done work can therefore go unnoticed and uncorrected. There is, in that sense, a certain tolerance built into the vastness of society. But if such tolerance is taken advantage of, and others are purposely duped or victimized, society's judgment will be severe and the punishment harsh.

In contrast, one might have a good idea and work assiduously to make it succeed, only to find that society pays little attention. It is easy, at such times, to conclude that the world is indifferent and to feel isolated and hopeless. But there is no need for such pessimism. For every thousand who do not understand or see, there will be a thousand who do. Therein lies the warmth of society.

Inasmuch as society can be both cruel and kind, we should strive always to be humble, to maintain hope, and to press onward along the path we have resolved to take.

A Game You Must Win

Work is a game you have to win. Every step is a win-or-lose situation. But do we approach our day-to-day work in such a competitive spirit?

The small slips and errors we make in the course of our regular work are not the sort of mistakes that put our lives at risk. We tend to let them slide, and at the end of the day, they remain and are gradually forgotten. Our standards may slacken, one day following the last, today the same as yesterday, without any reason for remark. But nothing useful comes of this inertia—no innovation, no originality. And where there is no tension or discipline, there is also no gratification or fulfillment.

As long as life is going smoothly and without accident, we carry on from one day to the next, but ultimately the smooth sailing does not go on forever. Conditions in the country, reflecting changes in the world, are in constant flux; we cannot ignore the trends of which our economy is a part. If we seek to attain true prosperity, we must pursue our work with courage and a competitive spirit.

Is this not a time when the difference between those who are really committed to the game and those who are not will be clear for all to see?

STAYING POWER

Patience and fortitude are important in everything we do, but this virtue of *staying power* seems to be less valued today. One observes a tendency among people to throw up their hands and give up even at the slightest difficulty. When a situation goes contrary to plan, people seem to expend their energy on shifting the responsibility, abusing others, and blaming society.

It would be like criticizing the consumer, for example, when certain goods do not sell. Consumers, however, would pay no attention to such a charge. If goods are not attractive enough or services not beneficial enough, consumers simply will not buy them.

An entrepreneur has to have staying power. We need determination to accept the situation, devotion to revise the strategy, and efforts to build up the capacity to make the plan work. So when goods don't sell, we would first examine why, tighten our belts, and go to work to make or develop products with qualities that consumers would be happy to buy.

If the chassis of an automobile is strong and sturdy, the car will run for a long time with proper maintenance and repair; likewise, if our character as human beings has strong staying power, we can keep going through thick and thin. Fortitude is a virtue for our environment-conscious times; it assures our efforts will not be in vain.

6

Rebuild Your Confidence

■ □ ■

Happiness for ourselves alone
Is but small and transient.
We should commit ourselves, rather,
To a larger vision for our country, for our
*   world.*
We should build upon rich traditions,
Our strength and resources of human
*   character*
And our heritage of self-reliance
Forged over long centuries.
It is time to regenerate and rectify
Our politics, our economy,
Our education, our culture,
For a more vigorous democracy
And for ever-greater happiness
For the whole world.

■ □ ■

LEARNING FROM FAILURE

The old saying that goes "Fall seven times, get up eight" describes those resilient people who, no matter how many times they may fail, pull themselves dauntlessly back to their feet over and over. Life is long, and the world is a tough place to survive in; there will be failures and disappointments along the way. At times like that, it is good to have this model to aspire to.

It would be foolish, of course, to take the saying to mean that all one needs to do is to get up only after falling seven times. If you do not learn a lesson when you take the first fall, you will have gotten nowhere even after seven falls. We should strive to be the kind of person who learns a lesson with every fall.

To become that kind of person, we need to commit ourselves, whenever we tumble, to doing more than simply getting back on our feet. The usual use of this saying is as a synonym for the greedy and grasping, but as among the sages of old, there are

also many stories of those who found enlightenment after taking a fall or experiencing some misfortune. That is because they did not merely get up,
and they were not greedy; they were dead serious.

Rather than fearing failure, what we should fear
more is not taking life seriously. If we are in earnest,
even if we take a tumble, we will have the presence
of mind not to simply go on without thinking about
what happened.

We should all try to become serious enough to
do more than just get up after a fall.

Success and Failure in Their Place

If you attempt a hundred tasks and succeed in only
one of them, should you call that success or failure
overall?

All too often, because of the ninety-nine failures,
everything seems to go wrong, and we give up, lose
heart, and never try again. When that happens, it
is a total failure.

When you think about it, however, you have not failed all one hundred times; even if it was just one case, it did come out right, so it was a success. If you succeeded even just once, that could mean there was a possibility of success for the other ninety-nine attempts as well.

Looking at the situation that way gives us courage; it gives us hope. Rather than thinking less of the one success, we can see it as the precious foothold to confidence in challenging the other ninety-nine again.

Once you have come this far, you are close to success with everything; without doubt, you will achieve what you aim for. Everything depends on where you set your sights: whether you will find hope in a single success or give up in despair at the other ninety-nine attempts. Therein lies the line between success and failure and one of the guideposts on the way to prosperity.

THE PAPER-THIN DIFFERENCE

The difference between genius and madness is paper thin, they say, yet what a difference it is. We cannot disparage the importance of the paper-thin difference; after all, it is that slight difference that can produce a genius or a madman.

One can observe the same about human intelligence and foolishness. Wisdom and folly are very far apart, yet the line between them can sometimes be very thin. In other words, whether we consider a person wise or unwise can be determined by only the slightest difference in perspective. The way people view others is up to them, and all are free to see the matter in their own way, but since such slight differences in perspective can distinguish between wisdom and folly, success and failure, prosperity and poverty, we cannot be careless about the way we look at the world.

When we think about it, everything in our daily lives is determined by slight differences. Understanding the importance of such differences, therefore, is crucial and calls for an open mind. How

openly we can look at life holds the key to that subtle difference.

BETTER THAN ABSOLUTE CONFIDENCE

We are told to go out in the world, to proceed in life
always with absolute confidence. That may be very
well advised, yet upon careful consideration, there
is little in this world about which we can really have
unswerving confidence. It is really impossible.

In a world that is changing constantly, minute
by minute, and in which we have no way of knowing what the future holds, we would have no way of
choosing our path with utter confidence unless we
were somehow divine or omniscient. This is all the
more reason, so that we can avoid mistakes as much
as possible, that we should consider all the alternatives and think about the future deeply. Once we
have exhausted all perspectives and alternatives,
we will decide upon on what seems to be the best
option. We may still not be certain it is right but
conclude that we must do our best, gathering cour-

age and moving along steadily, urging ourselves steadily onward.

We may adopt what seems to be confidence, all the while behaving in quite a tentative fashion, for ultimately all we can do is to grope our way through life. We may not strike a bold or imposing figure, but rather than being carried away by a confidence we do not really feel, we can find the optimal path through life—at least one that does not harm others—by assuming a modest mien.

Through Thick and Thin

Gorged by waters from a fierce storm, the river rises, flooding the town and washing everything away. The town may seem to have been destroyed, but ten years later, such a town often turns out to be cleaner and more prosperous than a town that was never flooded nor harmed in any way.

At tremendous cost and after great hardship, never giving up to the difficulties suffered and filled with a determination to overcome the odds, the survivors put their heads together and worked harder than ever. In the end, they created a town that far outdid the towns that had not been flooded. Those towns were safe and ordinary; the flooded town had to struggle with all its might to survive. It made a big difference.

We would all hope to avoid natural disasters and misfortunes; we would far rather go through life without them. Nothing would be better than if life went along smoothly and according to our hoped-for plans, but in this world and with the paths we follow, rarely does life go that way. The unexpected can happen at the most unexpected moment.

We cannot afford, however, to simply accept both hardship and good times as they come. Rather, in both good times and bad, we should commit ourselves to using our brains and applying our brawn as best we can to make the most of the situation.

The Power Within Us

The path of life for some people may appear to stretch out smooth and wide; for others it seems to be a rugged road of many ups and downs. The way we see life differs greatly from one person to the next.

In our daily lives, we hardly think of life as going forward smoothly. It appears to be full of ups and downs and twists and turns. For every difficulty we tackle and overcome, another lies beyond. There is no time to gaze about or even catch our breath before we face the next challenge. Indeed, our daily lives are witness that this, in fact, is the nature of life itself.

One wonders, however, how the lives of human beings appear from the viewpoint of the divine. Could it be that, in the larger scheme of life, what appears to us to be constant turmoil and trouble is actually quite a smooth and even way? Have our lives, which ought to have unfolded without trouble, been rendered rough and tumble, up and down out of our own shortcomings and shortsightedness?

Eventually, we will see life for what it really is. In the meantime, we can merely make our way earnestly, as best we can. It is this commitment to the power within us that lights the path of our lives, whether the way be rough or smooth.

HARD AND RIGID IS BAD

If you huddle rigidly in a cramped place, your legs will soon ache and become numb. Your body becomes rigid, and it becomes difficult to move freely. Lacking the capacity for refined manners may be a problem, but being rigid is worse. We should strive to maintain a capacity for creativity and free and easy movement.

Rigidity is bad, whatever the context. Physical rigidity is not healthy, but mental inflexibility is worse. When the mind ceases to be supple, it no longer provides useful answers.

There are various ways of seeing the world, and there is no one way that is always valid and correct. We have to be able to adjust our perspectives depending on the time and the situation or place. When our minds become hardened, we lose this capacity to adjust our perspective. We become stuck in one way of seeing the world, and that limits our freedom of movement and judgment; we can become stuck in one place. When that happens, we cannot hope to achieve new growth or development.

The myriad aspects of the world are different every day; they are constantly changing. Their appearance today is different from how they looked yesterday. We are part of this process of change; we have to constantly adjust our perspectives to meet the new perspectives of each day.

We should encourage each other to avoid rigidity and open up our minds to see the world clearly and think flexibly.

THE WAY LIFE SHOULD BE

As life becomes less settled and people are caught up in the competition and the rapid pace of change, the grass begins to seem greener in other people's gardens. While we are toiling away, assiduously and seriously, others seem to get rich wherever they turn, taking it easy while making money hand over fist. We think we ought to be able to get lucky like that just once, but that is not the way the world works.

Human nature being what it is, we cannot be blamed for being tempted to think we can find a shortcut to wealth and happiness, but in truth, such notions are illusory. To think there is an easy way is to delude ourselves, for there is no other way than to work away, one step at a time, steadily and surely, toward your goal.

To think that anyone rakes in money without making any effort is naive. Some people may experience a windfall of this sort, but the situation usually does not last long. Easy money does not last. Ultimately, the cases of people winning easy money tend to be flukes and do not follow what we know to be common sense. To count on life going against common sense is simply greedy.

Greed is indeed the root of failure, to be avoided at all costs. We are safer heading steadily along the natural and sensible path.

The Wisdom of One

Even for the brightest and the best informed, there are limits to the wisdom at the command of one individual. Despite those limitations, we have to make our way through the long years of our lives, and inevitably we stumble a bit here, meander a bit there. As long as we are responsible only for ourselves, some ineptitude may take no toll. But inasmuch as we are part of society—in which many people are closely interlinked—a misjudgment or miscalculation on our part could hurt or inconvenience others. If we risk causing trouble for others, it is surely better not to try to rely on our own wisdom alone.

We should be quick to ask about what we do not understand or what we do not know. Even if we think we understand, sometimes it is wise to ask again, for another point of view.

"The wider your perspective, the less you will wander; the more attentively you listen, the less you will wander," goes the old saying. No matter what sort of person you are dealing with, if you are humble and respectful, you can gain unanticipated knowledge from the encounter. The wisdom of one becomes the wisdom of two. And this effect is duplicated: the wisdom of two can become the wisdom of three, and so on. This is how knowledge is pooled.

We should strive to put our minds together with others, rather than attempting to get along with only the wisdom of one.

THE SILVER LINING

In the long course of our lives, not everything is happiness and light. If there were no hardships and no worries and life went along in a pleasantly peaceful manner, all would be well, but ordinarily that is not the way life goes. Over and over, we face disappointment, desperation, and crises that stretch us to the limit.

These times in extremity are part of life. Only in distress, sometimes, do we realize for the first time the profundity of life; only in crisis do we finally perceive the richness of our social web.

Understanding the world intellectually is valuable, but firsthand experience can be even more important: you cannot know the taste of salt by reading about it in a book. We acquire knowledge in various ways.

Being pushed to an extreme can be seen as an invaluable opportunity to learn, body and soul. Such opportunities are rare and precious. Looking at hardship from this perspective can give us courage even in the most difficult of situations. It can give us renewed energy. New insight grows out of the change in our thinking that results. Misfortune becomes fortune. Behind the dark cloud, we see the silver lining and feel a sense of renewal. The way opens up for us to rediscover our strength and forge onward.

7

To Further Improve
Your Work

■ □ ▩

We should not focus our attention narrowly
On our own immediate needs,
But look twenty or thirty years hence.
We should seek an orderly freedom
In which individuals and organizations can
    work freely.
A world where all can make the best of
    distinctive traits
Is one where human beings and society
Are assured boundless growth and
    development.
By combining forces, our respective strengths
    complement each other.

> *Where help and support is needed, we can*
>   *help each other.*
> *Let us seek a free and broad-minded path,*
> *Concerned about our country and the whole*
>   *world.*

■ □ ■

THE MEANING OF
YOUR WORK

Any kind of work is valuable if it is needed by society. If an activity is not sought after by people in society, it does not stand as "work." The shoe shiner had a successful business as long as there were people on the streets who decided then and there that they wanted their shoes shined. If there were not such people, that kind of job would not have come into being.

We cannot indulge ourselves with the notion that we do our work for ourselves. Rather, we do it because we are asked to do so by society. Therein lies the meaning of work.

A person who is devoted to and enthusiastic about his or her work may be able to exercise some say regarding the way it is done, but if it is forgotten that the work being done is for society, it could be reduced to a selfish action that is done only for someone's personal interest and gain. How a person's work grows and evolves is up to society. We should develop our work naturally, in the directions sought by society.

What matters most is to pursue the work society has given us to do in a conscientious, humble, and careful manner. We should strive to respond to the demands of society with all our might. We should always be mindful of the meaning of our work.

BETTER WAYS OF WORKING

Work that brings sweat to the brow is important and should be valued. But to toil away, sweating forever and ever, is not smart. It is like walking a distance of 200 kilometers, as people were forced to do long ago, when you can take the train. Over the long years of history, people shifted from walking to riding in palanquins, then in carriages, and then in trains, and finally to flying in airplanes. Gradually, they made less and less use of their own legs to get places. In these shifts from one form of transport to the next, we can see the progress of human ways of life.

The worker who puts in an hour longer than anyone else is praiseworthy and should be valued as serious and hardworking. However, a person who works an hour less than he or she previously did but whose output has increased—that person, too, is praiseworthy, and the difference represents progress in the way people work.

Innovation is vital. Creativity and inventiveness are crucial. Hard work is precious, but we should strive to innovate and improve on the way we work. We applaud those who do the physical labor but also those who use their brainpower and technology to get the job done. It is not a question of slacking off or taking it easy. We should always strive to develop easier ways to work if we can thereby increase our productivity.

Innovation generates prosperity for society.

CAREFUL AND QUICK

Work that is done carefully, meticulously, with checking and rechecking, and is finished to the finest detail, is always important. Nothing great can be achieved if the small details are left untended. We should strive to give our closest attention to the details of a task, however minor.

To do a job with such extreme care that completion takes an excessive amount of time, however, may not be what is called for. For the artisans of old, time was in ample supply; they took pride in producing work of great perfection. In the premodern era, the finely worked results of an artisan's most painstaking skill were highly prized. Today time is money; the value of every minute, every second is valued and counted. Doing a job and making the customer happy therefore means not only doing meticulous and careful work, but also doing it as fast as it can possibly be done.

Neither fast and sloppy nor meticulous and slow is permitted. The master of work for today is one who can perform a job with care but quickly.

ESTABLISHING DISCIPLINE

You get up in the morning, wash your face, and perform your morning rituals. Your family joins you. Your day begins with a simple and sincere moment of reflection. In the evening, you repeat the ritual. It need not be formal, but by observing a set order of events each morning and evening, you establish a rhythm and rigor in your life. A certain degree of regularity is important in whatever we do. A life without any sort of regular rhythm falls into inertia: there is no motivation to work, no time set aside for good ideas to emerge, and good results are lost.

The same goes in business and in management. An enterprise run without rules and regularity will, in due course, collapse. It may hold up all right in good times but will topple quickly in case of recession. Just as the strongest embankment can collapse if it is full of ants' burrows, a big enterprise without rigor and rules will cave in. By establishing some rules in the small aspects of life, we can cultivate the resilience and strength to succeed in big tasks.

Discipline is important in cultivating rigor and regularity. We should strive to acquire discipline in daily life, for it serves us personally and prevents us from inconveniencing others.

We should do our best to discipline ourselves and establish a life with rhythm and rigor.

READING THE SIGNS

When you go to a shooting gallery, there is a monitor on duty who raises a flag every time you shoot. Depending on the position of the flag, you can tell at a glance whether you hit or missed, and whether your shot was off to the right or to the left. Correcting your aim accordingly, you try again. Practicing with the flag as your corrective, you can gradually improve. If the monitor weren't there, calling your shots, you could shoot a hundred shots and be firing into the dark, never knowing how effective your aim was and never improving your marksmanship.

Come to think of it, in the course of our work every day, there are in fact many such flags—figuratively speaking—being waved at us, offering us guidance and showing us how we are doing. Numbers are among the most visible examples of such signs, but there are also many that are invisible.

If we identify the invisible signs and carefully tally the results of our work each day, our work will surely improve, drawing on the valuable accumulation of each day. Our days are invariably busy, but we should train ourselves strictly to keep an eye not only on the visible but also on the invisible signs that tell us how we are doing.

NEVER LET GO

Children dog the heels of their parents. They are always clamoring for one thing or another, always underfoot, never letting us alone. Sometimes they can be an embarrassment, but we still dote on them. They make us happy; we never want to let them go.

The products we make ourselves, the goods we sell, the work we do, too, can be hard to part with; we are reluctant to just send them off, hand them over, and move on to the next task in purely businesslike fashion. If we are serious about manufacturing, conscientious about sales, and truly passionate about our work, we want to know what happens to our products, our merchandise, and the results of our work.

We not only want to know what happens to them at the time but also to follow them ever afterward, to keep up with them on and on. For a kitchen appliance, we would like to tag along into the customer's kitchen; for a heater or an air conditioner, we want to step into the person's living room; for an automobile, we would try to follow it onto the roads of other countries—never letting go in our eagerness to know its fate: Is it working well? Does it need adjustment or tuning or repair? Are there problems or shortcomings? Even if it might be a bit bothersome, the consumer is happy and grateful to know that the manufacturer is concerned about its products, that it is serious and sincere in its postsale service.

This is the spirit, at least, in which we should try to make products, sell goods, and perform services.

The Magnetism of Determination

A magnet attracts steel. The power of attraction is invisible but clear. The magnet naturally pulls steel toward itself.

In our work, there are various qualities that we try to cultivate, but surely the foremost is a sincere enthusiasm for what we do. Knowledge is important. Talent is important. But even without either of them, you could get the job done. With but minimal knowledge and little talent, if you were determined to complete the task, you would ultimately be able to accomplish the work well.

Even if a person cannot do a job personally, his or her sincere enthusiasm for the project generates an invisible power that draws people around. It works magnetically to mobilize the kind of support that is needed. And the job will be completed through the assistance and intervention of others.

Know-how and talent would be useless without passion for work. We should do our best each day. Each of us has something to contribute, pouring the best of the resources at our disposal into the job to be done.

DOING ONE'S BEST

In whatever we do, when we have worked whole-heartedly and put forth the best that we can, we seek a reward for our labors. We want to pat ourselves on the back.

Even when we have put in a long day, busy with many tasks, but worked hard and finished up, we feel relieved and, though tired, have a good appetite. We can relax, and even as we think back on the work completed, we are satisfied. We experience a kind of calm because we know we have done the best a human being can do and know the rest is "up to heaven," as the old saying goes.

In many tasks, we may feel we come up short, but if we have done the utmost within our power, we do feel comforted and happy. We are rewarded.

Nothing can replace that feeling; money cannot buy it. People who think money can buy it do not know the true rewards of work well done. They are people who do not know how to savor the pleasures of work. Such people are unhappy indeed.

Many people measure results on a scale of success or failure, but even more important is something you can only feel within your own heart: the knowledge that you have done your best.

The Truly Complete Job

You are asked to do a job, and you do it, just as you have been told. That is all very praiseworthy, but then the question is, Have you reported your efforts to the person who requested the work?

Some people believe that all they have to do is complete a job as requested. If it goes well and according to plan, they think they are finished. Others make it a rule, even if a job goes as ordered, to report the results, straightforward as they may be, thinking that it will reassure the person who requested the job. This is a thoughtful approach and can make a big difference. The difference between these two approaches can determine the confidence a manager places in the person asked to do a job.

In getting a job done, the knowledge and skill of the person asked to do it are both significant, but perhaps even more valuable is the attention given to detail and to what might seem like routine matters, to tidying up the job to every last minor detail— leaving nothing undone that should be done. Only when the constant and regular attention to detail and completion of routine matters are added to knowledge and experience will people have unshakable confidence in us.

PROFESSIONALISM

A professional is someone who makes his or her living by pursuing a certain occupation. To put it another way, in any occupation, if one receives money from others for performing some service, one is thereby a professional. One is no longer an amateur.

In the worlds of the arts and sports, the distinction between professional and amateur is strict. If the product of artists or athletes is not of a professional level, audiences or spectators will not pay money to see them. Consumers do not pay money out of the kindness of their hearts. Achieving the status of a professional, therefore, is not easy, and the effort required to maintain one's professionalism is likewise tremendous.

The professional is never indulged. Upon leaving school and taking up employment, one begins to receive a salary. Once you start receiving a salary, you have, in a sense, become self-sufficient. You have joined the professionals. You are no longer an amateur. In that sense, like a performing artist or a competitor in sports, you must train yourself and maintain the high standards of a professional.

Aspiring to the standards of a professional and maintaining them should be our constant concern.

8

To Further Expand Your Business

■ □ ■

Rules and laws are important.
In order to live in peace and contentment,
We should strictly follow them
And make a clear distinction
Between what we must do and what we must not do.
Only when both adults and children bear this distinction in mind
Will our politics, business, culture, and education
Follow the steady development suited to the world of our century.

■ □ ■

SHIFT YOUR PERSPECTIVE

You can climb Mt. Fuji from either the west or the east. If the trail on the west is in bad condition, you can take the path from the east. If the path on the east is hard to follow, you can take the one on the west. You are free to change your path, depending on the time and the conditions. You can get into difficulties if you insist on always sticking to the same approach, and if you struggle too hard regardless of the situation, you may find yourself at an impasse, as if you were trying to move the mountain. Better to leave the mountain alone and shift your far-more-movable self; then you will discover a new path stretching before you.

In whatever you are doing, if you find yourself unable to go forward, you have to change your perspective. Sometimes we are hardly aware that we tend to cling to a particular way of looking at life, forgetting that there are other ways, and then conclude that there is no way out. We have become rigid to the point of forcing ourselves into an impasse.

We can free ourselves from such rigidity and strive for a broad-mindedness that will allow us to change our perspective. Clinging to any one approach will make us prejudiced in what we say and do. Before we conclude that a situation is hopeless, we should try changing our perspective. If the view from one place isn't good, we should try another and another until we eventually find what is the truly right path. This is the meaning of trial and error, and those who know how to try, over and over, will never find themselves at an impasse. We should all set out in search of the path to prosperity in that spirit.

THE VALUE OF BUSINESS

Life is a long and complex journey during which human beings can easily get lost. Religions have long served to provide wisdom and guidance, showing people how to navigate the perils and find bounty and joy in life. Over the millennia, religions have offered people salvation, purification of earthly life, and a rich variety of spiritual culture.

The power of religion is tremendous. Based in the strong belief in the salvation of human beings, religion works actively to give society what it seeks. And in return for the happiness the faithful thus receive, they support their religion with donations, alms, and other forms of material support.

Business can be seen as having some of the qualities of religion. The true purpose of business is likewise to provide that which society desires through the best service that can be offered, thereby elevating the standard of living and enhancing the convenience and richness of daily life. As long as the price is fair, such businesses, too, provide people with happiness. Their revenues should be in accordance with the happiness they render. It is worth taking a moment to think about the value of business and how it compares with the value of religion.

THE REAL PRIORITIES

The way a wrestler competes has to be fair and square, or fans will be disappointed, and the popularity of the sport will suffer. The competitive nature of the sport means that winning is important, but a wrestler cannot stoop to any foul means for winning and hope either for victory in the true sense or to keep a good reputation. Competition, in other words, involves not just the winning or losing but the way you win and the way you lose.

The same goes for the management of a business. No matter how large the concern or small the firm, it is an enterprise that has to show some results. Everyone involved has to work hard and do his or her best, but proceeding recklessly, intent only on producing results regardless of how others are affected, prevents the activities of the enterprise from contributing anything of value to the society. For those running a business, then, two crucial issues are the content of what the enterprise produces and its use of right and proper methods for achieving results.

For all people in the world to attain prosperity, our top priority is to succeed, difficult as it may be, in a manner that is right and proper.

HAVING FANS

Fans are a blessing. In sumo, for example, fans choose the wrestler they like. When he wins, they celebrate with delight; when he loses, they mourn and commiserate. There is nothing to be won or gained by being a fan; fans champion a competitor they favor in some way, and they cheer him on for those qualities.

Not only for competitors in sports but also for people in performing arts, fans are important. Celebrities work hard day and night to further enhance their performances, the better to respond to the expectations of their fans. By encouraging improvement among athletes and performing artists, fans thus play a role in the development of the sport or the art in question.

When you think about it, not only celebrities but all of us have our fans. Individuals, shops, companies—all have their own followers and admirers, and directly as well as indirectly, these fans provide tremendous support.

Recognizing that we do have fans is something we ought to think about anew. And we ought to be thankful for their presence and treasure them, working harder to improve those parts of ourselves that we know appeal to those who support us. That is the key to the prosperity of each individual, shop, or company.

GRATITUDE

The prices may be the same, but people will naturally tend to patronize the shop that takes good care of its customers and is thoughtful and conscientious about its services or merchandise. Few customers will return to an establishment where they get little attention and where common courtesy and respect is not observed.

The shopkeeper who sees customers to the door with an almost-reverent feeling of appreciation and gratitude runs a shop that is successful. If the customer is sufficiently respected, the quality of the goods and the level of the service will naturally rise. Care with details, personal attention, and thoughtfulness make all the difference.

The successful shop, moreover, does not keep customers waiting. No matter how good the product and courteous the service, in our time-is-money era, there is a limit to people's patience. The shopkeeper who is sufficiently attentive will be aware of a customer's desire for speed and always ready to respond to it.

Service rendered with kindness, quality, and quickness, as well as a spirit of reverence—a business thus run, no matter where it is, will be successful.

SEEMINGLY SMALL MATTERS

Critical reflection is necessary in whatever one tries to do, and as said many times, it is especially important in business. Even the humble peddler of roasted sweet potatoes tallies up his take at the end of the day and figures out how he did. If his wares sold well, he considers why many sweet potatoes sold; if they didn't, he also contemplates the reasons why. On that basis, he considers how much stock to put in tomorrow, how to better regulate his oven, and how he can improve his service, and he encourages himself to try hard the next day. This is the secret to the good business these peddlers enjoy.

Thus it is all the more important for businesses that handle many products and deal with massive numbers of customers to value the practice of taking stock and reflecting on their practices each day. Without the sort of reflection and reassessment that is a daily habit even to a peddler, how can any enterprise hope to develop and grow?

It is a seemingly small matter, but even such small matters that allow one to carry on business as usual can require considerable practice. Surely, what leads from the ordinary to success is the steady accumulation of little, routine actions we hardly ever think about.

Learning from the Enemy

If we are convinced that we are right, we may be forced to conclude that someone who voices a different view is wrong in all matters. We are on the right side; the other is on the wrong side—to wit, the enemy—and thus despicable. We want to conquer the other and wipe it off the scene.

Some may say this impulse is only human and cannot be helped. Yet there is actually quite a bit we can learn from those whom we think are against us and stand in our way.

Should the opponent move this way, we will counter it that way; if it comes along that way, we'll confront it this way. Faced with some adversary, we scheme and calculate to optimize our advantage. And gradually we progress. We think we are coming up with all these ideas on our own, but in fact we are learning from our opponents. The prodding of the other makes us rack our brains and exercise our imaginations. Isn't this learning from the enemy?

Simply destroying the enemy is pointless. If you destroy your opponent, you'll have no one to learn from, and you'll make no progress. Rather, you may find it useful to let a conflict of interests serve its purpose, each side learning from the other and both moving along the path toward progress and improvement. We should pursue, in other words, a path of both conflict and harmony.

This follows the laws of nature; it is the law of coexistence and the natural law that leads to prosperity.

The Danger of Too Much Success

We would all rather succeed than fail—that is obvious enough. But trouble lurks for those who have experienced success for every plan that they have laid. Gradually, such people become overconfident and begin to boast of their ability, and then they cease to listen to others, no matter what they do. Nothing could be more dangerous.

Confidence, of course, is good; without some degree of confidence it is better not to set out on any sort of plan. The confidence we develop, moreover, should be qualified, not absolute. There is nothing in this world, after all, that is certain or that we can be absolutely sure of. All certainty is relative; everything is tentative and subject to change. Some people find it difficult to understand this, and even a little success will convince them that they can be absolutely certain they know what to do. As long as we keep in mind that nothing is certain, we will remain humble and capable of listening with an open mind to the views of others.

For even the most brilliant and capable, therefore, it is safer to be successful only about two times out of three. Failure that translates into humility and lessons learned is what makes human beings grow.

No one wants to go through a series of failures, but a series of successes, too, can harbor risks.

With a Passion

Management is fascinating. Work itself is fascinating. No matter how many years one engages in management or any other work, one never exhausts the endless possibilities or uncovers all its mysteries. There are any number of approaches to the work and any number of ways to carry it out.

Over the centuries, you might think that every possible apparel design had been explored, yet even today, the supply of original designs continues— new ones coming out all the time, one replacing the next, as progress goes on. With the subtlest change in ways of thinking, new designs sprout up all over. This is the way it is in management and in any kind of work.

But without a passion for management or for work, the fascination would soon fade. It was someone's determination to find a way to reach a second-floor or a higher level that led to the invention of the ladder or the stairway. Passion was the mother of invention.

You might think it takes genius to invent a new product, but actually it is that verve, that determination to find a solution. This is the same in management and in business. We should approach the fascinations of management and of our work with this sort of passion and determination to succeed.

THE SPIRIT OF GOING INDEPENDENT

In the merchant houses of old, there was a custom of dividing the "shop curtain" (*noren*) to allow a senior clerk to become independent and build a business relying on the name of the master's shop. A clerk who had worked for many years and accumulated a respectable amount of experience was given the opportunity to run a business of his own with the blessing of the former employer. This custom, called *noren-wake*, may survive among some businesses, but it no longer exists within the business world.

Production as well as sales is today conducted by large concerns, and the old, personal style of dividing a business has died out with the rise of new corporate and management practices. The whole concept of branching out on one's own and starting a new business with the blessing of a former employer is difficult; in most cases, managers end up working their whole careers as an employee of a large company.

With the progress of mass production and consumption today, it is only natural that the scale of manufacturing and marketing should shift to large corporations. It is unlikely that this trend will be reversed. Somehow, however, we should strive to preserve the spirit of independence that was fostered by allowing employees to set up their own businesses under the custom of *noren-wake*. Even if we are employees of a large company, we can, within the context of performing within the position we are assigned, think of ourselves as independent. Insofar as we are responsible for that job, we are the independent master of our own operations.

It is essential throughout our careers to maintain the integrity and spirit of the independent entrepreneur.

Money with Real Value

Suppose someone hands you a stack of money. How easy it is to spend, and you let it run out of your hands without thinking; before you know it, it has all been used up. Only then do you realize that you don't have much to show for the money spent. The value of the money was somehow lost.

Money is money, but when it is money that we have gained through the sweat of our brows, we do not let it run out easily. We use it with care and prudence, and then the value purchased by the money glows brightly.

Money was meant to circulate. The money you might now possess is yours just for the time being, but in actuality, it belongs to the country you live in. To use such money carelessly is equivalent to squandering the resources of the country.

Using money to the best advantage of its value is one of our major responsibilities as citizens in our society. It is our duty. To use money properly, it ought to be money that we have earned by our own hard work. We should not receive money that we have not earned by the sweat of our own brows, and we should not borrow it.

This should be our rule—in our private lives, in the management of our enterprises, and in the administration of our countries.

Following Through

A spacecraft is launched, heading for the moon. With a roar and trailed by the rocket's plume, it shoots up high into the sky, and before we know it, it disappears into the distance, far out of sight. Various devices, however, keep track of its flight, enabling the launchers to observe it constantly until it reaches the moon, thousands, tens of thousands of kilometers away. Every step of the flight is tracked and observed.

Indeed, the tracking, the results are all part of the significance of a space flight. If the event were not tracked, it would have no meaning. To launch a spacecraft off into outer space without a trace would be nothing but squandering money.

The same is true in society and human affairs. People order others to perform some task. They give directions, request tasks to be done. But it is meaningless if they simply send off orders, issue commands, and make requests without following up on them, and the results would be minimal.

Wherever orders are issued, they should be followed up on. Everything should be checked back on, made responsible, reported on. Those who order work to be done are responsible for making sure, no matter what it takes, that the work has in fact been completed.

Follow-up is not easy for those who have been put to work or for those who have to do the follow-up. More care may be needed even than by those who track a rocket's flight, and more perseverance. Those who do the follow-up as well as those who are followed up on must cultivate the resolve and the courage to resist the tendency to leave any given task unresolved and unfinished.

9

To Cultivate a Spirit of Independence

■ □ ■

What is it that you seek?
What do you want to be the result of your
labors day to day?
What is it that your country sees as the
objective of its progress?
If you believe that you have important
qualities to offer,
Then every politician, every person in
business,
Every company employee, professional, and
guardian of the household
Should use these qualities to the full in
performing their duties,

Putting aside the habit of dependence on
   others,
To keep the country on an even keel in the
   coming century.

■ □ ■

LEARNING SELF-RELIANCE

The parent lion pushes its cub down the cliff, an act of fierce but instinctual purpose. But in spite of the harsh treatment, the young cub does not falter; it does not give up.

The cub scrambles for its life, it concentrates its whole being, and although it falls back over and over again, it gradually climbs, one crevice at a time, out of the ravine. As it pulls itself upward, it learns the importance of self-reliance; alone, on its own strength, it experiences body and soul that it can make its own way even out of adversity. It is in this way that a cub develops the inherent courage and strength of the lion.

Some harshness is necessary in acquiring independence. It requires courage. It is sometimes so bewildering that one feels like crying out. You may cry, you may wail, but in the next moment, you must work up new courage to find your way.

Indeed, harshness is the precious guidepost of self-enlightenment on the path to an unshakable self-reliance. Have courage. Brace yourself.

In a rapidly changing world, conditions are not easy, even for a country. It goes without saying that the situation for each individual is severe. Every day, we should be ready to meet the challenges of self-reliance.

Don't Be Selfish

Human beings have a tendency to think life will go the way they want it to. Rain clouds may be gathering, but some imagine selfishly that they can elude getting wet. We are all free, of course, to indulge ourselves as much as we want, as long as we have the fortitude to put up with the consequences. When it rains, everybody gets wet; that is the way the law of nature works. But if we put up an umbrella, we will not get wet; that, too, is the natural way of the world.

So if we cultivate a good insight into the laws of nature and courageously follow them, we can take whatever we want for granted. However, if we think that we will escape getting wet when it rains, in due course we will encounter trouble. If such consequences do not trouble us, that is fine—as long as we do not blame it on others. Some people cause unhappiness for themselves and others by blaming their misfortune on others. Such selfish behavior should be discouraged.

We are all busy, but we should take time now and then to quietly observe how our words and actions measure up against the laws of nature. It is worth considering whether we are asking too much and what we can do about it.

Consider Your Blessings

Human beings often act in a quite arbitrary fashion; they feel resentful and envious of others for that which they do not have while in many cases remaining oblivious to the good fortune they already enjoy. The slightest annoyance can prompt them to complain or harbor dissatisfaction, even though no sort of wisdom or wit can come from such grumblings. Because of this tendency, people of fortunate circumstances can, without ever realizing it, be the ruin of their own good fortune. Indeed, it is quite absurd. If they had simply felt gratitude for the blessings they had and worked enthusiastically and hard with that gratitude in their hearts, they would have made all manner of clever discoveries and found happiness in life for themselves and others.

Recognizing our good fortune is, after all, not easy to do. The sages of ancient times wrote tomes enjoining people to appreciate their blessings, yet how few people there are who can take such words seriously. They might understand the idea in their heads, but it does not really resonate in their hearts. Such is the nature of humanity.

We need to train ourselves to know our blessings. To directly understand how lucky we are, we need to add a new measure of introspection to the routine of our daily lives.

IT'S GOOD TO HAVE FEAR

Children fear their parents, the shop clerks fear their boss, the employees fear the company president, and the president fears the consumer. Then, too, there is fear of the gods, fear of Allah, fear of the Buddha. We all have someone or something we fear. It is good to have something to fear. That is what, in fact, sustains and supports us.

You might think that since your body is your own and your mind is your own, you should not have much difficulty controlling yourself of your own accord. Yet reining yourself in does not even go as well as with a horse or a bull. The difficulty of taming human impulses, indeed, has challenged the wisdom of sages since ancient times.

All the more do we ordinary folk have difficulty keeping ourselves in line. Our best bet has been to have something to fear and to control us out of the fear and rebuke delivered by that fearful presence.

Nothing is more dangerous than knowing nothing at all to fear. We might sometimes think we should be able to do without it, yet, depending on one's perspective, there is some benefit, some advantage to having something to fear.

Don't Take It Too Easy

After coming home from a hard day's work, nothing is better than sitting down in your own living room. You can relax, both mind and body. You might even become so relaxed that you find it hard to move at all, prompting complaints from family members. This may be forgiven as long as you are at home in your own living room; you just have to be careful of getting this relaxed when you are anywhere else, lest it cause inconvenience for others and get in their way.

If you get too complacent in your position in the company, forgetting the mission you must perform and becoming too distracted by your own concerns, then you will be doing more than just causing inconvenience for all those around you. Not only will your own work not get done, you will delay the work of those around you and even get in the way of the development of society itself.

Certain positions and roles are given to us so we can smoothly perform the duties arising from the positions through our mutual cooperation. We should do what we are supposed to do to make the business function more efficiently and progress further, lubricating the wheels of social advancement and contributing to the prosperity of all. That being the way life is, we really cannot afford to sit and take it easy.

It would pay for us to think again about our work and the role we are expected to play for the company and society at large.

Ever Mindful of Trouble

When business is brisk and society is affluent, we are content and wish that circumstances would continue that way forever. But for all of us, where there are happy days, there are always stormy and windy days as well.

As far as business is concerned, there are booms and recessions; prosperity rarely lasts indefinitely. That is the nature of human society; that is the way of the world. Yet when our world grows calm and business picks up to a certain extent, living standards improve, and so-called tranquility prevails, we are likely to forget the realities of the world and of human life as the days go by.

If that is all that happens, we are fortunate. But then, should a typhoon or hurricane strike or the ripples of recession arise, we may well wonder why we allowed ourselves to be so complacently content with the tranquility of days past.

Even when times are peaceful and quiet, we ought always to be poised to deal with whatever change might suddenly be visited upon us. As the old saying goes, "In times of peace, be mindful of war."

As aware as we may be of this wisdom, we must do more to remind each other to put it into practice.

DEVOTION TO WORK

Smart people, ironically, are often susceptible to failure. Examples abound. Bright people tend to let their own intelligence get in the way, preventing them from absorbing themselves in their work and getting their jobs done. Their great knowledge and understanding notwithstanding, they often cannot complete the simplest task properly and end up inconveniencing the client or customer.

There are those, by contrast, who are capable of plunging enthusiastically into whatever the task, even if it is of the utmost simplicity. People like this are intently focused. Even a job that might seem dull and trivial is for them something to be cherished, and they devote themselves to it body and soul. Naturally, such a person's knowledge and experience come into service in the job and come alive through its performance. People who can work like that are often very successful.

We should remember that whether a job succeeds or not is actually secondary. Our first priority should be to focus our energies, body and soul, and concentrate on the work as something to be cherished for itself. That is the only way that anything can come out of one's work.

Before we bewail our own inadequacies and dissatisfactions in our work, we should first ask ourselves if we are wrestling with our work with real devotion.

KNOW THYSELF

Whatever the battle or challenge, the often-heard advice is to "know your enemy" or "check out the competition." When one country is defeated in war by another, it may first be reproached for not knowing its enemy well enough to win. This is certainly a valid observation, but there is a lesson to learn even before that.

You must know *yourself*. You must be able to look at and reflect upon yourself.

Knowing your opponent is no easy task, but knowing yourself is perhaps even harder. Not knowing the opponent fully, you might be able at least to hold your own in the match, but not knowing yourself will invariably lead to defeat. In every battle and every defeat, the cause of failure will always lie in not knowing yourself.

The same can be said of everything in human affairs. More often than you might think, the inconveniences and troubles you encounter are of your own making. To save us all from the regret of finding that we are the cause of our own failures, we should all cultivate the awareness that we need, above all, to know ourselves.

ACUTELY AWARE

Sometimes we think we are trying very hard on a job, and then something happens that affects us deeply, making us acutely aware that what we had thought was hard work was still far from adequate.

Experiences that affect us to our very core are valuable; we should be grateful for them. If we hope to complete some task carefully and without error, whether it be momentous or minuscule, the sense that the endeavor is important to us very deep down in our soul is basic.

Today, constructing even a small building equipped with all the conveniences of modern technology can take a year and a half. It is interesting to consider that the grand and resplendent Osaka Castle, despite being erected in an era—the late sixteenth century—without the conveniences of modern construction equipment, was completed in a mere year and a half. Behind this monumental achievement was the awareness on the part of those engaged in the construction that they might pay for poor or inept work with their heads. They threw themselves into the work with the seriousness of those who have staked their lives on their work. This is a rather extreme example of what can be achieved when we take our work very seriously.

Whatever we do, we have to carry on working, one day at a time. We have to do our best. But it is good to take time to consider whether our work reflects an awareness deep within us of its importance.

RETURN TO NORMALCY

When fire breaks out, anyone is likely to panic. You may tread on other people's toes as you try to put out flames, carry valuables to safety, and seek people's help. Some extraordinary behavior would be allowable in such an emergency. For several years after World War II ended, an emergency prevailed far greater than any ordinary fire. People acted and thought the way they do in crisis situations. It couldn't be helped in those days.

Once an emergency is over, however, life has to return to normal. Once the fires are put out, you have no excuse for treading on anyone's toes to get a task done. And you cannot take it for granted that people will help you out when you are in trouble. Once the situation is back to normal, you are expected to think and act in the spirit of normalcy—that is, in a calm and balanced fashion.

The question today is whether we have really returned to normalcy. Our lives have long since become peaceful and affluent, but it seems as if many of the ways of behaving and thinking that we indulged in during times of crisis remain deeply rooted in our society and institutions.

It takes courage to return to and maintain the spirit of normalcy. But having that courage and keeping a critical eye on ourselves is the starting point of our path as human beings.

All in Life Is Linked to You

Nothing would be easier than to blame others for anything and everything bad that happens. We could shift the responsibility to others and act as if we knew nothing about whatever might go wrong. But if everyone took that attitude, each trying to fob off responsibility on the other, what would the world be like?

Any excuse is possible; there are countless ways to escape responsibility and burden. We may have no legal obligation. In the context of society, however, which functions through the interdependencies of people in daily life, there is nothing that is totally unrelated to ourselves, nothing for which we are not in some small way responsible. Even that which we might think unconnected to us in any way is, by various circuitous circumstances, linked to ourselves. Inasmuch as we are linked this way to all that is around us, we have to think carefully about ourselves and the ramifications of our own actions.

The instinct to lay the blame for misfortune on others may only be human nature, but in fact it is the habit of the cowardly and weak. A society made up of only people like that could not possibly achieve true prosperity for everyone nor genuine peace. We must all try to cultivate in ourselves, as adult members of society, the capacity to recognize our responsibilities and the courage to accept them.

THE DUTY TO TEACH

Human beings are admirable and amazing. They are capable of feats that no other living creature can perform, and they invent new goods as well as ideas. No wonder they have become the lords of creation.

But if a human baby were left alone at birth and not taught how to be a human being, its life would probably not be much different from that of a wild animal. Since time immemorial, even the sage, no matter how great, was once an unknowing and innocent child, who learned from parents, teachers, and others with prior experience. Only on that basic learning does the sage build wisdom; without the guidance of such people, a sage would be a charlatan.

Without teaching, nothing new can happen. Teaching is the important obligation of human beings who come before toward those who come after. Are we resolutely performing this important task? Do we display the deep devotion and commitment such a vocation merits?

We ought to be more enthusiastic teachers. We ought to be more enthusiastic in teaching and more humble in being taught. We should all know that without teaching, nothing new is born.

WILLINGNESS TO LEARN

We may believe our ideas are our own and our knowledge something we acquired on our own, but in fact, all of it is taught to us by others. Without being taught, without learning, a human being would have hardly a notion in his or her head. Small children learn from their parents, students from teachers, juniors from seniors, and so on. Your own ideas and thoughts are the result of this tremendous amount of learning. So naturally people who produce good ideas and good wisdom are those who are at the same time good at learning.

When you possess the spirit of a good learner, everything around you is your teacher—the silent trees and rocks, the drifting clouds, the innocent child, the stern lecture of a senior, the good advice of a junior. This is because everything in the universe quietly pulses with the laws of nature, and so does everything in the long history of humankind, no matter how small, no matter how old. Valuable human insights and experiences are reflected in these constants.

There is something we can learn from everything. We should be ready and willing to learn from anything and from anyone. Only when we are thus willing can we learn something new and be able to come up with good ideas. The spirit of learning is the first step toward true prosperity.

THE MOST ORDINARY OF DEEDS

When we wake in the morning, we wash our faces. We sweep the path before our doorway and sprinkle water to settle the dust. This is our ordinary and unremarkable routine.

If you receive a present, you say thank you; if someone goes out of his or her way for you, you express thanks for their trouble; if your house or office becomes cluttered, you tidy up. There is nothing complicated or debatable about it. Dogs and cats don't bother with such deeds, but for human beings, they are just basic, ordinary responses that we hardly think about.

Yet some people are in the habit of coming up with some reasoning or excuses to avoid even such ordinary tasks. If self-serving, arbitrary reasoning prevails, there would seem to be no reason to tidy up, to wash one's face, or to sprinkle water at the front stoop. It would be difficult to do such ordinary actions and routines, and the yardstick for deciding or doing anything grows hard to find. This situation prevails all too often in this day and age.

The source of this problem lies in searching for the path that serves self-interest, yet I believe that the path to true prosperity for ourselves and others is to be found in the most ordinary places, in the most obvious concepts upon which everyone generally agrees. We do not need to make life complicated.

We should think again about what is most important. Just as water naturally flows from high to low, just as summer is followed by autumn, all in life follows nature's laws. We, too, should try to follow the path that nature has given us.

THE CAPACITY FOR RESPECT

When schoolteachers are made light of and students feel no respect for their professors, those who teach feel little incentive to instruct, and students little motivation to study. The loss to society is tremendous.

Only if we respect our teachers for their calling and honor the person who humbly follows the teaching profession can we truly learn from everything that is taught and grow from it.

We should treasure our parents, respect our superiors, honor our seniors, and serve our benefactors. Respect is due not only to teachers and parents, but to those who do good work, to those who toil in obscurity. For everything, anywhere in the world, if we but have this spirit of respect, we will find that which deserves it.

Respect is an essentially human sentiment, and only humans have the capacity to recognize value that they can respect; it is part of our inherent character. Those who make the best of this capacity, finding that which they can respect and enriching themselves and others through that respect, can constantly grow and excel.

We should accept and embrace this human capacity for respect. By enhancing our sense of respect, we can enrich our appreciation of each other.

TOUCHED TO THE HEART

If we are deeply touched by whatever we hear, whatever we see, then each and every thing we see and hear becomes an integral part of us, and we feel myriad sensations and emotions. When we are thus deeply touched, others' tears move us to tears. We feel the happiness or the sadness of our mundane world with infinite depth and poignancy.

Some people live uneventful lives without any particular thoughts or experiences that arouse deep emotions or for which they might stake their lives. No matter what they see or hear, they are not much moved, and everything seems to be someone else's affair, of little relation to themselves.

Perhaps one's life can be this way, yet in a way it is a life sorely lacking in flavor or zest. For human beings, in the long course of life, it is important to know what it is like to be touched to the heart.

This is not just an individual matter; with an empathetic heart, we should look around us anew. As we think of our own country and the world, we should think again about the future, with the empathy to sense within ourselves the feelings of others.

10

For the Sake of
Your Own Fulfillment

■ □ ■

Is it only a dream
That we could have a simple meeting of
*   minds,*
And that we could join hands in the search
*   and pursuit*
Of prosperity, peace, and happiness?
When we are too serious about what we do,
Conflicts of interest are likely to occur.
But if we become aware of common goals
We can achieve a close harmony and a robust
*   power,*
And then it will not just be a dream.

■ □ ■

KNOW THE TRUTH

Human beings, depending on their perspective, can put up with just about anything. They can endure the direst hardship, the heaviest burdens. They even know how to be cheerful in the face of misfortune or discomfort, and they are capable of finding gratification in what is difficult or burdensome. It all depends on the attitude, the perspective they adopt. The reason that the same human being can be both devil and saint is the result of this power of attitude. If we can harness the power of attitude, then there should be nothing in life that is hopeless or impossible.

Anyone who wants to achieve a proper attitude or perspective in life, however, must know the truth and must teach the truth. The reality of existence must speak to that person.

Affection is important, but if we are so influenced by sympathy or pity for someone that we do not speak the truth, that cannot be called true affection. The greatest misfortune is ignorance of reality, not knowing what is true or real.

Human beings are great; when they confront the truth, they can rise above circumstances and achieve peace of mind. We should all strive to see the world correctly and keep open minds, always telling the truth and letting each other know the truth.

ROLLING AROUND IN LIFE

As a metaphor for life, I often recall a scene that was once part of the urban landscape in Japan. To wash potatoes, people used to pour sacks of them into a large vat of water. Young fellows wielding thick poles would then stir them around vigorously, and as they were sloshed around, the big ones and small ones floating up and sinking down, appearing and disappearing, and bumping and rubbing against each other, the mud fell away. Washed this way, the potatoes at the top of the vat might not always stay at the top and often would sink to the bottom, and the potatoes at the bottom weren't always on the bottom and often would be pushed to the top, but in the end they all got cleaned.

Indeed, we often feel like potatoes being stirred around in a great vat, bumping into each other in various ways and being swept up, down, and around by the circumstances of human life. The big and the fat ones are not always at the top, and the small and skinny ones are not always at the bottom. The ups and downs have the effect of bringing out the best in people, polishing them as human beings. What with all the buffeting, moreover, those who happen to be on top cannot afford to be too arrogant or proud, and those who happen to be down below cannot just languish in pessimism and self-pity. All need to try to keep an open mind, be humble and tolerant, and keep going with a hopeful spirit.

When we find ourselves tempted by either arrogance or depression, it might be useful to keep in mind the image of being rolled around in the vast potato vat of life.

THE VALUE OF AN END

We know very well that just as life has its beginning, so it must have an end. This is as obvious as that there is a beginning and an end to each year. We know that we don't have to start worrying about the end of the year and try to take care of everything before we get there, yet as the year-end approaches, we invariably find ourselves rushing from one task to another as we hasten to tidy up loose ends. We want to enjoy the satisfaction of settling our debts and completing our assignments before the year's 365 days come to an end.

Likewise, we know our lives will eventually be over. When death is not far away, we know it is already too late to panic about what is unfinished, yet we cannot help feeling anxious, wanting to tidy up our affairs. The end of one year leads into the beginning of the next, but the end of life is different.

When you are working to finish tasks at the end of one year, you know that once that turning point passes, the beginning of the next opens out before you. In the case of life, the end is the end. It is more final.

In the face of unbending circumstances, however, human beings are at their most earnest. Being able to surmount difficulties by flexible thinking or ardent effort is all very good, but there is merit, too, in a situation that you cannot overcome, no matter what you might do.

Every person is different. Every situation is unique. Life is full of cares. But knowing that at the end of life there is that one line that will not budge is one truth that we should always keep in mind.

Everyone knows that life could be over at any moment, yet it is these certainties that we all know so well of which we must keep reminding ourselves.

YOUR MISTAKES

Human beings are not perfect, and none of us can hope to perform without ever making a mistake. Miscalculations and failures are all part of life. That being said, it is important that we should always, under any circumstances, be ready to humbly accept our mistakes, and we should possess the strength of character to be willing to take responsibility for them.

One of the reasons we admire the samurai of old, too, is that they practiced an ethic that forbade them from escaping the consequences of their own mistakes. They recognized when they were at fault, and they knew what they had to do without complaining, even if it meant retiring or dying. There is something we admire in the behavior of a human being who is disciplined and mature.

To live by such a model of honesty and integrity may be asking a lot, but people today are amazingly frail and brittle by comparison. I do not know whether they lack sufficient training or personal discipline, but I often meet people who not only will not admit to their faults but try valiantly to shift the blame to others. People like this will fail to recognize when they should take responsibility and withdraw from their position. Before they know it, they are desperate, hurting themselves and hurting others. This is no way to achieve prosperity, happiness, or peace for anyone.

We should make it a rule to humbly accept our mistakes and be ready to take full responsibility for them. This rule is one we should try daily to cultivate within ourselves.

THE VIRTUE OF DILIGENCE

Even without the devastation of fire or natural disaster, the vastest accumulation of wealth could disappear overnight. We know that all material goods will eventually pass away, and indeed their duration is fleeting.

The skills we master and the habits we acquire, by contrast, we do not lose as long as we live. In the end, it is on our skills and abilities, our customs and habits that we can depend.

We should try therefore to equip ourselves with some useful skills and some good habits. One of the most valuable habits, I would say, is diligence. Diligence brings happiness, creates trust, and generates wealth; it is one of the most important human virtues. And, inasmuch as it is a virtue, it takes unremitting effort to acquire.

Just as a sumo wrestler can grow strong only by continuing steady and serious practice, the only way to achieve the habit of diligence is through the accumulation of daily effort. Only when the effort accumulates does diligence become a habit that can truly become a virtue. We should all do our best to cultivate the virtue of diligence.

THE LIMITS OF WISDOM

There would seem to be a great divide between people who are very smart and people who are dull-witted, yet if we look at them in the grand scheme of nature, we can see that both intelligence and dull-wittedness have their limits. Even the brightest, smartest person is less wise than the gods or the Buddha, and even the dullest person is smarter than a cat or a dog.

We are indebted to nature for 99 percent of ourselves, body and mind. The percentage of ourselves that we can determine by our own free will is really quite tiny. Within that small margin of human wisdom unfolds the immense diversity of personalities and a variety of lifestyles. No matter how we may boast of a modicum of wisdom or how we may deprecate ourselves for our folly, it is still quite a small matter in the larger scheme of life. Both prideful boasting and self-pity are sheer nonsense.

There is only a paper-thin difference between the smart and the stupid. Even in a person of great intelligence, one can observe naïveté, while even in ignorance, one often finds sharp wits.

We should not allow ourselves to be perturbed by such a very small difference. We must only strive to live out our lives calmly, steadily making our way forward.

ON IMITATION

Tokugawa Ieyasu (1543–1616) was an amazing man. He might not be much of a hero to some, but he was the samurai general who stabilized the whole country after a long period of chaos and in 1603 built a regime that kept peace in the country for nearly three centuries. So he was a person of outstanding ability in certain ways. Recently, there was something of an Ieyasu boom, and novels about his life became bestsellers.

But just because Ieyasu was great does not mean that he is someone we ought to try to imitate. Ieyasu followed the path he did because he was who he was, and even someone smarter or more capable than Ieyasu could easily go astray by following his example too closely.

Learning, of course, begins by imitating, as we can easily see by watching children. But an eggplant cannot grow on a gourd plant. Persimmon seeds grow into persimmon trees; plum pits grow into plum trees.

Every person is different; we cannot be Ieyasu. Like the persimmon and the plum, each person has his or her own characteristics. The important thing is to recognize what your own characteristics are. We ought to think for ourselves. If you want to imitate someone, it ought to come after that.

SELF-IMPROVEMENT

Zen training is rigorous. If, as you sit in meditation, your mind wanders and you squirm on your knees, a blow on the shoulder from the priest's bamboo cane helps bring back your concentration. You cannot complain that it hurts or is painful.

Surrounded by strict rules in a Zen retreat, even the way you eat is prescribed. Those who have grown self-indulgent and lax would not last a moment in such an environment. Yet when you live in such a strict environment, as time passes, you find that it ceases to feel harsh. Discipline is only difficult when you think of it as harsh. When, however, the rules become part of your daily life, then you find that they are no longer confining. It is when a person ceases to feel that these rules are confining that he or she begins to exude the beauty of a polished human being.

Human beings are by nature great. They are to be admired. But the natural qualities will not shine out if left neglected. People may be inclined to take the easy way out, but if they follow that inclination day after day, all that would be revealed would be our human failings.

To hone and polish the beautiful qualities of our humanity, we ought to improve ourselves to the point where discipline does not seem harsh.

LEARNING FROM EXPERIENCE

Suppose you decide you want to learn to swim and, having access to an outstanding swimmer, you request him to give you lectures explaining how it is done. You could listen to such lectures regularly, for three years in a row, be instructed in the minutest detail about swimming and all of the knowledge related to swimming, and happily master it all as an intellectual exercise. But would you actually be able to swim?

No matter how perfectly and completely you might master the information the great swimmer imparted to you, if tossed into the water, you would almost certainly find yourself floundering. The ability to swim cannot be acquired in the classroom alone.

There is no substitute, after all, for getting into the water and actually moving your limbs. You have to know what it is like to swallow water and sputter until tears come to your eyes. Sometimes it takes a near-death experience to really learn how to swim.

But in the end, you will learn how to float and how to swim. That is the precious reward of experience. It is when the textbook is put into practice through actual experience that knowledge comes alive. We should eschew the illusion that all we have to do is listen without taking action.

Keep Moving Forward

If you keep moving forward, you will unexpectedly find a path, and that is not just limited to situations when you are walking in the country or hiking in the hills. You may stop and feel satisfied with where you are, but if you move onward, you may find a new place that turns out to be better than where you were previously.

We often experience this in vivid ways in various corners of our daily life. You might not do this yourself. Some other people, who are not satisfied with the way the world is, believe there ought to be a better way, and they constantly strive to find a better way.

This is the way humankind has proceeded along the path of progress and development over the long centuries of history, by trial and error, moving ahead. And this is the way we will continue to advance, endlessly into the future. That is why human beings are great.

We ourselves are but one small frame in the long drama of human history. All the more, we should not easily succumb to the status quo or to complacency, but should constantly move forward every day in the hope of finding a better path.

II

For the Country
to Prosper

■ □ ■

We should always try to keep in mind that
We are all citizens of the same country,
And we are the sovereign people who must
     choose and decide
The direction in which the nation should go.
We should carefully and forthrightly examine
What is needed for the prosperity of not just
     our nation, but the world,
And think what is important for our peace
     and happiness as a people.
This is what we must do to make a country
That is worth working for and that can take
     pride
In an effective and genuine democracy.

■ □ ■

THE PATH OF A COUNTRY

People are all very different; everyone has a different kind of life, and the paths people follow are infinitely varied. Whatever path a person follows, no matter how quiet or out of the way it is, each person has to break his or her own unique path. And it is never easy. Each and every one of us must direct our will to this end the best we can. The path will not open up when we sit idly and wait, nor will it open up if we leave matters to others.

Even more difficult is opening up the path of a nation. No matter how earnestly we strive to make a way for ourselves as individuals, if the way does not open up for the whole country, everything we have built up will be but a castle in the sand. We might think that "someone will do something," but that is not the way the world works.

Surely the path of a nation is much the same as the path of the individual. It will not open up when we sit idly and wait. We will not find it by leaving the matter to others. Rather, just as we can find our own path by thinking hard, together with others, so we can find the path for our country.

In a democracy, this is the task we must set out to achieve—and indeed, we can do this precisely because we are part of a democracy. This is an aspect of life we should take time to reflect on.

ARE YOU READY?

How do you respond to a crisis? Can you keep your wits and steady your nerve? Are you ready to respond as calmly as you ordinarily do, and with the same kind of resolution and good judgment? I think we would all find this quite difficult. As the days go by without incident, we tend to grow careless, and when one day we suddenly face a crisis, we find ourselves stunned and lose all our normal resolve and good judgment.

When you think about it, however, our readiness and resolve is constantly being tested in day-to-day life. Living as we do on streets constantly buzzing with traffic, we can face danger the moment we step out our front door. Surviving in that milieu demands that we be constantly "ready."

Indeed, in everything about our lives, in many forms, and at every shifting moment, we have to be vigilant, on our guard. We have to watch for signs of danger ourselves; whether we are ready for whatever may come any moment is up to us. This attitude is all the more important in Japan today, in the face of constant changes taking place in social and economic affairs that parallel shifting trends in the world as a whole. We should all try to be as ready as we can.

LIVE BY YOUR CONVICTIONS

The merchants of old treasured two things: the shop's code of conduct and the *noren* curtain emblazoned with its trademark or crest. Stories tell that merchants would risk their lives to safeguard these revered components of their business that had been passed down to them from earlier generations.

They were proud of the shop code passed down to them and stood by it with conviction, sometimes with their lives. *Hagakure*, the eighteenth-century work that was a kind of bible of the samurai code of honor, declared that when forced to choose between life and death in a situation, the samurai should choose death. This may seem a little extreme in our day and age, yet a similar ethic was the source of the merchant's backbone.

Times are different. People think differently than in the past. But the value of living by a code—of sticking by your convictions—has not changed. Indeed, I am often struck that nothing is more precious in succeeding in business than faithfulness to one's principles, one's code of conduct. If statesmen lack principles, they will ruin a nation. Without principles, an entrepreneur will ruin a business, and a shopkeeper will quickly lose clientele. At no time is this more true than today.

We should establish correct principles to guide our country, principles our business can take pride in, and principles that will keep our shop or enterprise on an even keel—principles that will keep ourselves and others moving resolutely forward. Therein will be found true prosperity for ourselves, our enterprises, and our nations.

IT'S YOUR BUSINESS

Comedians come in all sorts and range from the virtuoso to the mediocre. A skillful comedian can keep an audience convulsed with laughter with lines that, delivered by an inept one, would be neither interesting nor funny. Listening to an amateur trying to sound funny is boring and a waste of time. Given the content is the same, what makes the performance so different?

A successful comedian has a distinctive style, a particular talent for being funny. And a professional jokester is practiced and inventive. Between the pro and the amateur, there is a difference in passion, dedication, and study. All these distinctions make a world of difference.

If you are listening to a comedy skit, all that is at stake from a bad performance is the time wasted; when it comes to the governing of a country, however, the matter is more serious. The territory, the people, the wealth, and the resources all being equal, a fundamental difference in the fortunes of the nation and the happiness of the people will result, depending on the attitude of politicians and the way they govern. What applies to the nation is exactly the same for the management of society, the running of a business, or the coordination of an organization.

This is not somebody else's business. It is our own business. Realizing that it is our own business, we should think again about the way we govern, the way we run our corporation. And we should reflect quietly upon ourselves as citizens.

Peace and War

Peace and war are inherently distinct and separate, and both in word and in fact, they are complete opposites. Peace is peace, and war is war.

Recently, however, there has been strange talk of "wars for the sake of peace"—and not only talk. The battles launched in the name of such wars have been flamboyant indeed. I suppose the arguments in support of such wars may have their own logic, but no matter what the rationale, that which is inherently one thing cannot be another.

Everyone in the world today knows from personal experience the awful tragedy of war; they certainly know enough not to be fooled by fallacious arguments that war is waged for the sake of peace. People know that war ought to be avoided as much as possible by making assiduous and serious efforts while peace still lasts.

Is it not about time that we all show that we have grown up? That in order to get along, we need not engage in childlike flurries of fisticuffs? We ought to be doing our best to speak peaceably to each other and considering together how we can best secure a peaceful prosperity for all.

This is a matter that is very close to home; it applies to our everyday lives.

CORDIAL CONVERSATION AND HARD WORK

Especially after World War II came to an end, people enjoyed widespread freedom of speech, and the world became in many ways a better, easier-to-understand place as a result. At the same time, such a clamor of voices has arisen, advocating one position or another, that the once-admired quality of keeping silent and working hard has been left by the wayside. I would not go so far as to say that all discussion necessarily gets in the way of prosperity, yet it seems to me this situation calls for some serious reflection.

The better the engine in an automobile, the quieter it is. It hums quietly but accelerates powerfully. If the engine is poor, it putters and clanks, making all sorts of loud noises, and before the engine can pick up any speed, it sputters and dies.

People may froth at the mouth and posture all they will, but heated argument rarely gets anyone anywhere. It is actually a bit unsightly, like the bad engine. We should endeavor rather to be like the good, well-lubricated engine, keeping our explanations and arguments to a minimum and moving our points forward calmly in the course of cordial conversation. That, indeed, is the kind of discussion that is useful in achieving prosperity in the world.

Discussing opinions calmly and getting down to work—this is an attitude to aspire to both as a country and as citizens, the better to assure our engines keep humming smoothly.

GETTING THE MESSAGE

The mechanisms of the human body are marvelously intricate and ingeniously designed. Even the most advanced communications satellite, with all its complex devices, cannot measure up to the mysterious handiwork of nature that is the human organism. It could be described, depending on how you look at it, as a re-creation of the mysteries of the whole universe.

The body is a complex and vast world in itself. Yet when a pin pricks the tip of one extremity, the brain gets the message immediately. The entire human frame is networked with a finely developed nervous system that reports even the slightest itch or twinge to the brain instantaneously. This is what allows us to respond quickly and appropriately to the situations we find ourselves in.

And then there are the organizations created by human society: shops, companies, associations, and federations, from sovereign states and regional unions to the largest of them all, the United Nations. If one were to poke any of these at the bottom rung, would the message be quickly transmitted to its top echelons? Would the organization be able to respond in a flash, the way the human body does? There is much talk about streamlining and improving performance, but what is really needed is a mechanism that is capable of quickly processing messages from outlying parts and responding immediately.

We should consider this matter, in our companies and our shops, as well as in the states and larger organizations of our world.

THE WORK OF GOVERNING

Whatever the work you do, it functions to help us all coexist and survive. One job is linked to another job and thus to many other jobs, and our world goes around as a result of all these links. So, to do a job only according to our own whim and will could end up causing trouble for others; such a self-centered way of working is not ethical either. The job we perform is work that has been assigned to us, but at the same time, it is not just our own work.

Government is a form of work that is directly linked to the citizens of a country. The quality of the work can quickly affect the fortunes of all the country's people. One might think, therefore, that the work of politicians would be highly respected and well remunerated.

In actuality, however, politicians are often the target of jokes and caricatures. On a certain television program, when asked by the announcer, "What do you want to be when you grow up?" an elementary school child said innocently, "I can't be a politician, I guess, because I'm not good at fighting and quarreling."

Those who would laugh off such a remark are undermining the very source of their happiness and good fortune. No country where politicians are treated lightly, or where they are not respectable and respected, can prosper.

Who is responsible for this situation? Does it lie with the people who chose those politicians for office? Does it lie with the politicians themselves?

SEEK FIRST WITHIN ONESELF

"When trouble descends, all you can do is pray," goes the saying, and human beings do have a tendency, when they are really perplexed, distressed, and at their wit's end, of finally resorting to prayer. "Please, please, hear my prayer," we plead to whatever our god or buddha, for deliverance from our plight or to get what we desperately need. The gods and buddhas have their work cut out for them.

Such may be human nature, but I cannot help thinking that we tend to seek and to ask too much, to rely too much on others. The proper nature of prayer, I should think, is to straighten yourself before your deity—resolving to correct those traits within yourself that may not be quite right by your own effort. Not to ask, not to seek, not to beg—the shape of true piety is to rectify yourself of your own power.

We would do well to cultivate the same attitude in our daily lives. Are you not asking too much of others? Are you not relying too much on others? We should strive as much as possible not to depend on others but to discipline ourselves and do the best we can. What applies to us as individuals also applies to organizations and to the state, the nation itself. Therein lies the true form of autonomy and independence for us as human beings and for our country as well.

RESPECT THE MASSES

The masses are ignorant, so what the ignorant masses think is irrelevant; what is needed is a great and wise leader, who will take the reins of government and control the country. That is the most desirable form of rule.

There was once a time when this conviction held sway in the world, and some still cling to it even today. Indeed, for a long time through history, the masses may have been unlettered and uninformed. And certainly because of that, many dictatorships and tyrannies came into being, plunging already unhappy people into even greater distress.

But history has advanced, and humankind, too, has progressed. Today the masses are well informed and discerning, and they are also very fair. Anyone who fails to recognize that the masses are no longer ignorant not only misinterprets the meaning of democracy but is an obstruction to the nurturing of democratic government—and is probably digging his or her own grave.

To repeat, the masses—the public—today are extremely sensible and fair. They should be trusted and their views made the foundation of democracy. The true mission of democratic government is above all service to the masses. The very essence of democracy, that service is the starting place for the prosperity of a nation.

THE BENEFITS OF DAMS

It rains, drenching the mountains, and the water seeps into the earth and forms rivulets, streams, and rivers, flowing out through the land, creating fertile plains before emptying into the sea. As long as the flow is used skillfully, the land prospers, but if something goes wrong, raging waters may cause flooding, or lack of rainfall may devastate crops. This is the result of just letting the water flow and not using it with careful thought.

Now consider the dam. We can dam the flow to form a reservoir of water that can be used in effective ways. When we know we have plenty of water, we can let the waters flow through; when we have little, we can store it up. This is a lesson that human civilization has learned.

Just as reservoirs are useful in rivers, so they are in our daily life. Having reserves is good both materially and mentally. There is nothing intelligent in a life of uncontrolled consumption and wastefulness.

In the same way that we build big, strong dams for great rivers and small reservoirs for small streams, as needed under the circumstances, so individuals can put to use the information they have to form various dams to regulate their lives.

The principle applies not only to individuals' lives, but in business as well; reserves in corporate management are highly to be recommended. Even more valuable are such reserves on the level of the management of a country. They will support the genuine and stable prosperity of a nation and its people.

THIS GOOD COUNTRY

When the flowers bloom, the sun shines brightly, and the sky is a dazzling blue, colorful banners, festive sights, and the merry voices of children in the distance herald the coming of spring, the beginning of the planting season. It is the season of renewal and hope.

The seasons follow the year around—the warm months, the rainy months, the blisteringly dry months, the cold months—in the cycle shared since time immemorial. We embrace the land and country we know: not just the landscape and its culture, but also the countless landmarks and treasures collected over its long history. We treasure, too, the inborn character of its people, their diligence and conscientiousness.

Ours is a good country; there are not many other countries like it in the world. So we want to make it an ever-better country and live in harmony with others, in lives that are affluent in both tangible and intangible ways. When you are blessed, if you do not know that you are blessed, it is as if you had nothing at all. Let us reflect again upon the good of our country and give ourselves a new chance to take pride in it.